Cambridge IGCSE®

Physics

Laboratory Practical Book

Heather Kennett

HODDER
EDUCATION
AN HACHETTE UK COMPANY

Safety checked but not trialled by CLEAPSS

This text has not been through the Cambridge endorsement process.

® IGCSE is the registered trademark of Cambridge International Examinations.

Answers can be found at www.hoddereducation.com/cambridgeextras

The Publishers would like to thank the following for permission to reproduce copyright material:

Questions from the Cambridge IGCSE Physics paper are reproduced by kind permission of Cambridge International Examinations. Cambridge International Examinations bears no responsibility for the example answers to questions taken from its past question papers which are contained in this publication.

Photo credits: **p.1** © sciencephotos / Alamy; **p.7** © Ian Poole/iStockphoto.com

Every effort has been made to trace all copyright holders, but if any have been inadvertently overlooked the Publishers will be pleased to make the necessary arrangements at the first opportunity.

Although every effort has been made to ensure that website addresses are correct at time of going to press, Hodder Education cannot be held responsible for the content of any website mentioned in this book. It is sometimes possible to find a relocated web page by typing in the address of the home page for a website in the URL window of your browser.

Hachette UK's policy is to use papers that are natural, renewable and recyclable products and made from wood grown in sustainable forests. The logging and manufacturing processes are expected to conform to the environmental regulations of the country of origin.

Orders: please contact Bookpoint Ltd, 130 Milton Park, Abingdon, Oxon OX14 4SB. Telephone: (44) 01235 827720. Fax: (44) 01235 400454. Lines are open 9.00–5.00, Monday to Saturday, with a 24-hour message answering service. Visit our website at www.hoddereducation.com

© Heather Kennett 2015
First published in 2015 by
Hodder Education
An Hachette UK Company
Carmelite House
50 Victoria Embankment
London EC4Y 0DZ

Impression number   5 4 3
Year   2017 2016

Cover photo © robertkoczera – Fotolia

Typeset in 9.5/14pt Frutiger LT Std 45 Light by Integra Software Services Pvt. Ltd., Pondicherry, India

Printed and bound by CPI Group (UK) Ltd, Croydon, CRO 4YY

A catalogue record for this title is available from the British Library

ISBN 978 1 4441 9219 3

Contents

Experimental skills and abilities

Experiments

1 General physics

2 Thermal physics

3 Properties of waves

4 Electricity and magnetism

5 Atomic physics

Past exam questions

Skills for scientific enquiry

The aim of this book is to help you develop the skills and abilities needed to perform practical laboratory work. We start by introducing the apparatus and measuring techniques that you will use most often.

Then we show you how to make and record measurements accurately. Methods for handling the observations and data you have collected will then be described.

Finally we discuss how to plan, carry out and evaluate an investigation. You should then be ready to work successfully through the experiments and laboratory activities that follow.

Using and organising apparatus and materials

In an experiment you will first have to decide on the measurements to be made and then collect together the apparatus and materials required. The quantities you will need to measure most often in laboratory work are mass, length and time.

- What apparatus should you use to measure each of these?
- Which measuring device is most suitable for the task in hand?
- How do you use the device correctly?

Balances

A **balance** is used to measure the mass of an object. There are several types available.

- In a beam balance the unknown mass is placed in one pan and balanced against known masses in the other pan.
- In a lever balance a system of levers acts against the mass when it is placed in the pan.
- A digital top-pan balance, which gives a direct reading of the mass placed on the pan, is shown in Figure 1.
- The unit of mass is the kilogram (kg).

Figure 1 A digital top-pan balance

- The gram (g) is one-thousandth of a kilogram:

    1 g = 1/1000 kg

    $= 10^{-3}$ kg

    $= 0.001$ kg

How accurately do your scales measure?

- A beam balance is accurate to the size of the smallest mass that tilts the balanced beam.
- A digital top-pan balance is accurate to the size of the smallest mass which can be measured on the scale setting you are using, probably 1 g or 0.1 g.

Ruler, micrometer screw gauge and vernier scales

Rulers, micrometer screw gauges and vernier scales are used to measure lengths.
- The unit of length is the metre (m).
- Multiples are:

    1 decimetre (dm) = 10^{-1} m

    1 centimetre (cm) = 10^{-2} m

    1 millimetre (mm) = 10^{-3} m

    1 micrometre (µm) = 10^{-6} m

    1 kilometre (km) = 10^{3} m

A **ruler** is often used to measure lengths in the centimetre range.
- The correct way to measure with a ruler is shown in Figure 2, with the ruler placed as close to the object as possible.

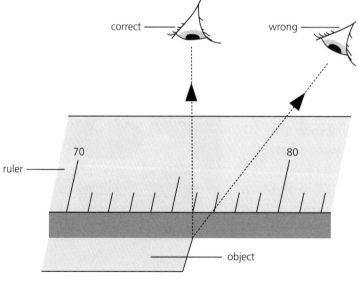

Figure 2 Using a ruler: the reading is 76 mm or 7.6 cm. Your eye must be directly above the mark on the scale or the thickness of the ruler causes parallax errors. The accuracy of the measurement will be about 1 mm.

- When measuring extensions (of springs, for example), it is best to record the actual scale readings for the stretched and the unstretched lengths, and then work out the extension afterwards.

A **micrometer screw gauge** (Figure 3) can be used to measure small objects in the millimetre range.

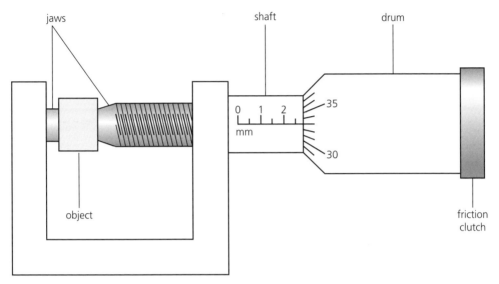

Figure 3 Using a micrometer screw gauge: the object shown has a length of 2.5 mm on the shaft scale + 33 divisions on the drum scale = 2.5 mm + (33 × 0.01 mm) = (2.5 + 0.33) mm = 2.83 mm.

- One revolution of the drum opens the accurately flat, parallel jaws by 1 division on the scale on the shaft of the gauge; this is usually 0.5 mm. If the drum has a scale of 50 divisions round it, then rotation of the drum by 1 division opens the jaws by 0.5/50 mm = 0.01 mm. A friction clutch ensures that the jaws always exert the same force on an object and over-tightening does not occur.
- Before making a measurement, check to ensure that the reading is zero when the jaws are closed, otherwise a zero error must be allowed for when a reading is taken. The measurement is accurate to 0.01 mm.

Some instruments, such as barometers and microscopes, have a **vernier scale** to enable small lengths to be measured, usually to 0.1 mm.
- One end of the length to be measured is made to coincide with the zero of the millimetre scale and the other end with the zero of the vernier scale (Figures 4a and 4b).

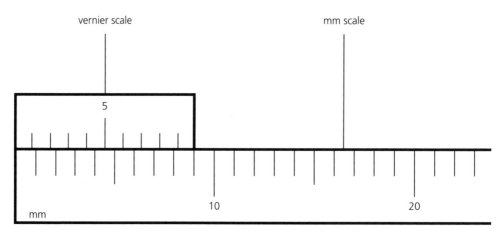

Figure 4a A vernier scale is a small sliding scale which is 9 mm long but divided into 10 equal divisions: 1 vernier division = 9/10 mm = 0.9 mm = 0.09 cm.

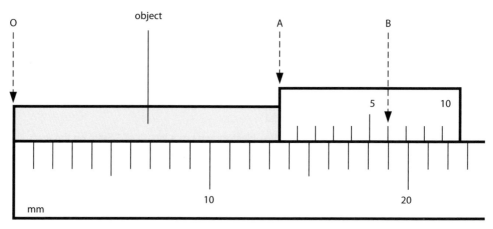

Figure 4b The length of the object is between 13 and 14 mm. The reading to the next decimal place is found by finding the vernier mark that exactly lines up with a mark on the millimetre scale. Here, it is the 6th mark and so the length of the object is 13.6 mm since:

$OA = OB - AB$
   = 19.0 mm − (6 vernier divisions)
   = 19.0 − (6 × 0.9) mm
   = 19.0 − 5.4 mm
   = 13.6 mm

How accurate are your length measurements?

- A ruler can be used to measure accurately to 1 mm, a vernier scale to 0.1 mm and a micrometer screw gauge to 0.01 mm.
- For very small distances, multiples can be measured and then divided to find an average value. For example, to obtain the average thickness of one page of a book, measure the thickness of 20 pages and divide your result by 20.

Clocks and timers

Clocks, watches and timers can be used to measure time intervals. In an experiment it is important to choose the correct timing device for the required measurement.
- The unit of time is the second (s).
- A **stopwatch** will be sufficient if a time in minutes or seconds is to be measured, but if times of less than a second are to be determined then a **digital timer** is necessary.

How accurate are your timings?

- When using a stopwatch, reaction times may influence the reading and an accuracy of about 0.5 s is the best that is likely to be achieved.
- For time intervals of the order of seconds, a more accurate result will be obtained by measuring longer time intervals and then dividing to find an average value – for example, to find an average value for the period of a pendulum, time 10 oscillations rather than one and then divide by 10.
- To measure very short time intervals, use a digital timer that can be triggered to start and stop by an electronic signal from a microphone, photogate or mechanical switch.

Changing measurements

- Take readings more frequently if values are changing rapidly.
- It will often be helpful to work with a partner who watches the timer and calls out when to take a reading.
- Pressing the lap-timer facility on the stopwatch at the moment you take a reading freezes the time display for a few seconds and will enable you to record a more accurate time measurement.
- For rapidly changing measurements it may be necessary to use a **tickertape timer** or a **data logger** and computer.

Some other measuring devices

Measuring cylinder

The volume of a liquid can be obtained by pouring it into a **measuring cylinder**.
- The unit of volume is the litre (l). Note that 1 litre = $1000\,cm^3 = 1\,dm^3$.
- Measuring cylinders are often marked in millilitres (ml) where 1 millilitre = $1\,cm^3$.
- The accuracy of the reading will be $1\,cm^3$.

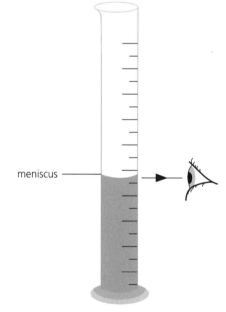

meniscus

Figure 5 When making a reading, the measuring cylinder should be vertical and your eye should be level with the bottom of the curved liquid surface – the **meniscus**. (For mercury, the meniscus is curved oppositely to that of other liquids and you should read the level of the top of the meniscus in a mercury thermometer or barometer.)

Protractor

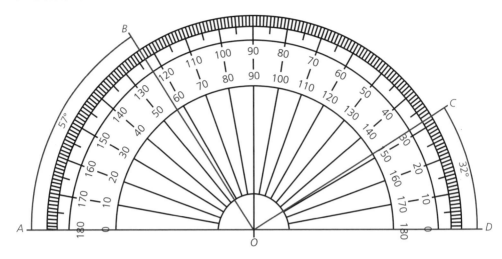

Figure 6 Using a protractor

A **protractor** is used to measure angles.
- When the angle between two intersecting lines *OA* and *OB* is required, set the horizontal (0–180°) line of the protractor on one of the lines (*OA*) and the zero dot of the protractor on the intersection point of the lines (*O*).
- The angle *AOB* = 57° can then be read off the inner scale of the protractor as shown.
- Similarly, the angle between lines *OD* and *OC*, angle *DOC* = 32°, can be read from the outer scale.
- The accuracy of the reading will depend on the size of the protractor; it is about 1° for a protractor from a school geometry set.

Ammeters and voltmeters

An **ammeter** measures electric current.
- The unit of current is the ampere (A).
- An ammeter should be placed **in series** with the device in which the current is to be measured.
- An ammeter should have a low resistance so that it does not change the current to be measured.

A **voltmeter** measures potential difference (p.d.).
- The unit of p.d. is the volt (V).
- A voltmeter should be placed **in parallel** with the device across which the p.d. is to be measured.
- A voltmeter should have a high resistance so that it does not change the current and hence the p.d. to be measured.

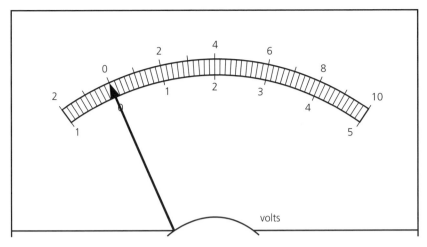

Figure 7 The display of an analogue voltmeter

- Figure 7 shows the display of an analogue meter with two scales. The 0–5 scale has a full-scale deflection of 5.0 V; each small scale division on this scale represents 0.1 V. The accuracy of the measurement will be about 0.1 V. For the 0–10 scale, each small division represents 0.2 V.
- As with rulers, the eye should be immediately above the pointer when taking a reading to avoid introducing parallax errors; if there is a mirror behind the pointer, the needle and its image should coincide when you take a reading.
- Check that the meter reads zero when there is no current; adjust the screw at the base of the pointer until it does.
- Digital meters such as that shown in Figure 8 allow different ranges to be selected and the display gives the measurement in whatever units have been chosen. The reading will be accurate to the last figure on the display, so for small currents and voltages it will be more accurate to use the mA or mV setting.

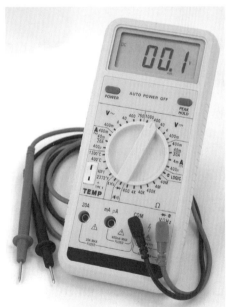

Figure 8 A digital meter

Tips for using meters in electrical circuits

- Construct circuits with the power switched off or battery disconnected and attach the voltmeter last.
- Check that meters are connected with the correct polarity and are set to their lowest sensitivity initially.
- Set the power supply output to zero before you switch it on.

Safety

Here are a few simple precautions to help ensure your safety when carrying out physics experiments in the laboratory.

- **Always wear shoes** – to protect your feet if a heavy weight should fall on them.
- **Turn off the power** – when connecting electrical circuits, ensure the power is turned off. When you are ready to take measurements, check the circuit and set the power to a low output before turning it on. Large currents can cause burns and electric shocks, and break sensitive meters.
- **Take care with hot liquids and solids** – set in a safe position where they will not be accidentally knocked over; handle with caution to avoid burns.
- **Protect eyes** – avoid looking directly into a laser beam or ultraviolet lamp; keep radioactive sources away from your eyes as radiation can damage them; wear eye protection when instructed.
- **Take care with toxic materials** – materials such as mercury are toxic; take care not to allow a mercury thermometer to roll onto the floor and break.
- **Tie back long hair** – to prevent it being caught in a flame, for example.
- **Put away personal belongings** – leave in a sensible place so that no one will trip over them!

Observing, measuring and recording

Having collected together and familiarised yourself with the equipment and materials needed for an experiment, you are now ready to start making some observations and measurements.

- It will be helpful at this stage to draw a clearly labelled diagram of the experimental set-up.
- You should also record any difficulties encountered in carrying out the experiment and any precautions taken to achieve accuracy in your measurements.
- Do not dismantle the equipment until you have completed the analysis of your results and are sure you will not have to repeat any measurements!
- What degree of accuracy will your measurements have?
- How many significant figures will your data have?
- How will you record your results?

Degree of accuracy

Make a list of the apparatus you use in an experiment and record the smallest division of the scale of each measuring device; this will be the accuracy of your measurements.

- For example, the smallest division on a metre rule is 1 mm, so the accuracy of any length measured with the ruler will be 1 mm.
- The degree of accuracy will be greater the longer the length measured:
  - For a measured length of 1 m = 1000 mm, the degree of accuracy will be 1 part in 1000.
  - For a measured length of 1 cm = 10 mm, the degree of accuracy will be 1 part in 10.
- Similarly if the gradations on a thermometer are at 1 °C intervals, the accuracy of a temperature reading will be 1 °C.

Significant figures

Every measurement of a quantity is an attempt to find its true value and is subject to errors arising from the limitations of the apparatus and the experimental procedure.

- The number of figures given for a measurement, called **significant figures**, indicates how accurate we think it is and more figures should not be given than are justified.
- For example, a measurement of 6.7 has two significant figures; the measurement 0.235 has three significant figures, the 2 being most significant and the 5, which we are least sure about since it could be 4 or 6, being the least significant.
- When doing calculations your answer should have the same number of significant figures as the measurements used in the calculation. For example, if your calculator gives an answer of 1.23578, this should be given as 1.2 if the measurements on which you based this calculation have two significant figures and 1.24 if your measurements have three significant figures.
- Note that in deciding the least significant figure you look at the following figure; if that is less than 5, you round down (1.23 becomes 1.2) but if it is 5 or above, you round up (1.235 becomes 1.24).
- If a number is expressed in standard notation, the number of significant figures is the number of digits before the power of 10; for example, 6.24×10^2 has three significant figures.
- If values with different numbers of significant figures are used to calculate a quantity, quote your answer to the smallest number of significant figures.

Systematic errors

Figure 9 shows part of a ruler used to measure the height of a point P above the bench.

- The ruler has a space of length x before the zero of the scale.
- The height of the point P = scale reading + x
  = 5.9 + x.
- By itself the scale reading is not equal to the height of P; it is too small by the amount x.
- An error of this type is called a **systematic error** because it is introduced by the system used to make the measurement.
- A half-metre rule does not have a systematic error because its zero is at the end of the rule.
- When using a rule to measure a height, the rule must be held so that it is vertical. If it is at an angle to the vertical a systematic error will be introduced.
- Check for any zero error when using a measuring device; if it cannot be eliminated, correct your readings by adding or subtracting the zero error to them.

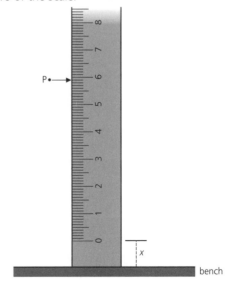

Figure 9 Introducing a systematic error into a measurement

Tables

If several measurements of a quantity are being made, draw up a **table** in which to record your results.

- Use the column headings, or start of rows, to name the measurement and state its unit. For example, in Experiment 1.1 (see page 20) you will use a table similar to the one below to record your results.
- Repeat the measurement of each observation if possible and record the values in your table; if repeat measurements for the same quantity are significantly different, take a third reading. Calculate an average value from your readings.
- Numerical values should be given to the number of significant figures appropriate to the measuring device.

Mass of pendulum bob/g	First measurement of pendulum length, L_1/cm	Second measurement of pendulum length, L_2/cm	Average pendulum length, L/cm

Handling experimental observations and data

Now that you have collected your measurements you will need to process them. Perhaps there are calculations to be made or you will decide to make a graph of your results. Then you can summarise what have you learnt from the experiment, discuss sources of experimental error and draw some conclusions from the investigation.

- What is the best way to process your results?
- Are there some inconsistent measurements to be dealt with?
- What experimental errors are there?
- What conclusions, generalisations or patterns can you draw?

Calculations

You may have to produce an average value or manipulate an equation to process your results.

Averages

Sum the values for a quantity you have measured and divide the sum by the number of values to obtain the average.

- For example, if you measure the length of a pendulum as 81.5 cm and 81.6 cm, then:

$$\text{the average value} = \frac{(81.5 + 81.6)}{2}\ \text{cm}$$

$$= \frac{163.1}{2} \text{ cm}$$

$$= 81.55 \text{ cm}$$

$$= 81.6 \text{ cm}$$

- The value has been given to three significant figures because that was the accuracy of the individual measurements on which the calculation was based.

Equations

When tackling physics problems using mathematical equations, do not substitute numerical values until you have obtained the expression that gives the answer in symbols. This reduces the chances of making arithmetic and copying errors.

- Equations frequently have to be rearranged to change the subject. For example, in the equation $y = mx$, the subject is y.
- To change the subject to x, we must divide both sides by m so that:

$$\frac{y}{m} = \frac{mx}{m} = x$$

or $x = \dfrac{y}{m}$

- If you have numerical values for y and m, you can now substitute them into the equation to calculate x. For example, if $y = 4.16$ cm and $m = 2.0$:

$$x = \frac{y}{m}$$

$$= \frac{4.16}{2.0} \text{ cm}$$

$$= 2.08 \text{ cm}$$

$$= 2.1 \text{ cm}$$

- The value for x is given to two significant figures because that was the lower of the number of significant figures for the values of y and m on which the calculation was based.

Graphs

Graphs can be useful in finding the relationship between two quantities.

- You will need about six data points taken over as large a range as possible to plot a graph.
- Choose scales that make it easy to plot the points and use as much of the graph paper as possible.
- Make sure you label each axis of the graph with the name and unit of the quantity being plotted.
- Mark the data points clearly with a dot in a circle or a cross with a sharp pencil.
- Join up your points with a smooth line or curve.

Straight-line graphs

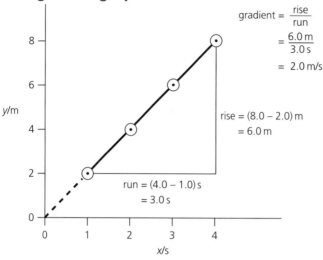

x/s	y/m
1.0	2.0
2.0	4.0
3.0	6.0
4.0	8.0

Figure 10 A graph showing that y is directly proportional to x

- When the readings in the table above are used to plot a graph of y against x, the continuous line joining the points (Figure 10) is a straight line through the origin (0, 0).
- Such a graph shows that there is **direct proportionality** between the quantities plotted: $y \propto x$.
- Note, however, that the line must go through the origin for the quantities to be proportional.
- If a straight-line graph does not go through the origin, one can only say that there is a linear dependence between y and x.
- When the readings (units omitted) in the table below are used to plot a graph of V against p, the continuous line joining the points (Figure 11) is a curve.

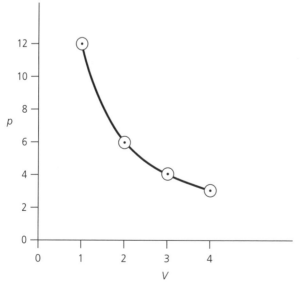

V	p	1/V
1.0	12	1.00
2.0	6	0.50
3.0	4	0.33
4.0	3	0.25

Figure 11 A graph showing V plotted against p

- If, however, $1/V$ is plotted against p (or V is plotted against $1/p$) then a straight line through the origin is obtained (Figure 12). In this case $1/V$ is proportional to p and there is an inverse proportionality between V and p:

$$\frac{1}{V} \propto p$$

or

$$\frac{1}{p} \propto V$$

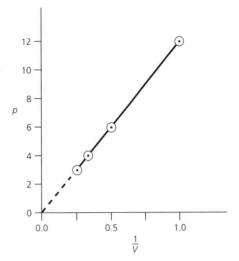

Figure 12 A graph showing $1/V$ plotted against p

Slope or gradient

- The slope or gradient of a straight-line graph can be determined by the triangle method shown in Figure 10.
- Use as long a length of line as possible to determine the gradient from the ratio of the vertical 'rise' to the horizontal 'run' of the triangle chosen.
- In Figure 10:

$$\text{gradient} = \frac{\text{rise}}{\text{run}}$$
$$= \frac{6}{3}\,\text{m/s}$$
$$= 2\,\text{m/s}$$

Errors

In practice, points plotted on a graph from actual measurements may not lie exactly on a straight line due to experimental errors.

- The 'best straight line' is then drawn through them such that they are equally distributed about it; this automatically averages the results.
- Do not force the line through the origin. Any points that are well off the line stand out and may be investigated further.
- If possible, repeat any anomalous measurements to check that they have been recorded properly or try to identify the reason for the anomaly.

Conclusions

Once you have analysed your experimental results, summarise your conclusions clearly and relate them to the aim of the experiment.

- State if a hypothesis has been verified; suggest reasons if your results do not, or only partially, support a hypothesis.
- If a numerical value has been obtained state it to the correct number of significant figures. Compare your results with known values if available and suggest reasons for any differences.

- State any relationships discovered or confirmed between the variables you have investigated.
- Mention any patterns or trends in the data.
- Identify and comment on sources of error in the experiment. For example, it may be very difficult to eliminate all heat losses to the environment in a heat experiment; if that is the case, say so. Mention any sources of systematic error in the experiment.

Planning, carrying out and evaluating investigations

Before you start an experiment it is important to define an aim and produce a logical plan for the investigation.

- You should identify the variables in the investigation and decide which ones to manipulate and which ones you should try to keep constant. The variable that is manipulated or changed is also known as the **independent variable**. The variable that responds and is measured is also known as the **dependent variable**.
- To discover the relationship between variables you should change only one variable at a time. For example, in Experiment 1.1 (see page 20), when investigating the variation of the period of a pendulum, we first keep the mass of the bob constant and record the period for different pendulum lengths; this will reveal how the period depends on pendulum length. We then keep the length of the pendulum constant and measure the period when different masses are used; this will show how the period depends on the mass of the bob.
- Once you know what you will need to measure, you can decide on the apparatus and materials to be used. You should ensure that your measuring devices have sufficient accuracy for the job required.
- Before you start the experiment, familiarise yourself with how to use the apparatus and develop a plan of work. It will be helpful to decide how to record your results; draw up tables in which to record your measurements if appropriate.
- Describe how you carried out the experiment under 'Method' in your laboratory notes; it is useful to include a sketch of the experimental set-up here for future reference.
- When you have obtained your results, manipulate data, draw graphs and carry out the calculations needed to fulfil the aims of the experiment.
- Then analyse your results and clearly state your conclusions from the investigation.
- Finally, evaluate the experiment and discuss how it could be improved. Could some things have been done better? If so, suggest changes or modifications that could be made to the procedure or the equipment used in the investigation.

Questions

1 What measuring device would you use to obtain values for each of the following?

(a) the volume of liquid in a coffee mug

....

(b) the mass of an apple

....

(c) the length of the pendulum of a grandfather clock

....

(d) the thickness of a wire

....

(e) the temperature of a cup of tea

....

(f) the time taken to run up 20 stairs

....

(g) the p.d. across a lamp

....

(h) the time taken by an apple to fall through one metre

....

(i) the angle that a beam of light is turned through by a plane mirror

....

(j) the current flowing in a resistor

....

(k) the dimensions of a textbook

....

2   How would you obtain a value for each of the following?

(a) the average thickness of a newspaper page

(b) the average time for one oscillation of the pendulum of a clock

(c) the average mass of a pin

3   Complete the table below by stating the typical accuracy of each of the measuring devices listed.

Device	Accuracy
metre rule	
vernier scale	
micrometer screw gauge	
stopwatch	
digital timer	
digital balance	
liquid in glass thermometer	
100 ml measuring cylinder	

4   Write the number 9.753864 to:

   (a) three significant figures ....

   (b) two significant figures ....

   (c) one significant figure ....

5   The power of a device is calculated from the equation:

   $P = IV$

   (a) If $I = 250 \times 10^{-3}$ A and $V = 8.0$ V, calculate P, giving your answer to the correct number of significant figures.

   (b) If $P = 60$ J/s and $V = 12$ V, calculate I.

6   The reading on an ammeter when no current is flowing in it is 2 mA. What is the true value of the current if the meter reads 26 mA when a current flows in it?

7   The measurements in the table below were obtained for the speed of a trolley rolling down a runway from rest.

Speed / m/s	Time/s
0.0	0.00
0.2	0.05
0.4	0.10
0.6	0.15
0.8	0.20
1.0	0.25

(a) (i) State the variables being measured.

....

(ii) Name a variable that is being kept fixed.

....

(iii) Complete the following table:

Manipulated (independent) variable	Fixed variable	Responding (dependent) variable

(b) Plot a graph of time on the horizontal axis and speed on the vertical axis.

(c) Calculate the slope of the graph.

(d) What can you conclude about the relationship between speed and time in this experiment?

....

....

....

1.1 Simple pendulum

Aim

To investigate the effect of length and mass on the period of a simple pendulum.

Variables

Complete Table 1.

Table 1

Manipulated (independent)	Fixed	Responding (dependent)

[1]

Apparatus

- ☐ support stand
- ☐ string
- ☐ 2 metal pendulum bobs of different mass
- ☐ stopwatch or clock
- ☐ metre rule
- ☐ scales

Procedure

Set up the apparatus as shown in Figure 1.

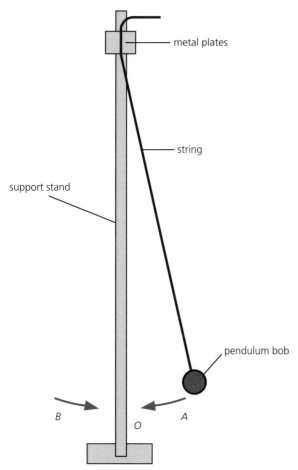

Figure 1

1 Measure the length of the pendulum from the point of support to the centre of the bob; repeat your measurement and calculate the average length.

2 Measure the time taken for the bob to make ten small angle oscillations; one oscillation occurs when the bob moves from $O \rightarrow A \rightarrow O \rightarrow B \rightarrow O$. Repeat the measurement and calculate the average time.

3 Work out the period, T, of the pendulum – this is the time needed for one oscillation.

4 Measure the mass of the pendulum bob.

5 Repeat steps **1** to **4** using a longer pendulum length.

6 Repeat steps **2** to **4** using a heavier pendulum bob and the same pendulum length as was used in step **5**.

Method

The length of the pendulum was measured from .... to

.... with .... [1]

Explain why ten oscillations are timed rather than one. [1]

....

....

....

....

....

....

Results and calculations

Complete Tables 2 and 3.

Table 2

Mass of pendulum bob/g	First measurement of pendulum length/cm	Second measurement of pendulum length/cm	Average pendulum length/cm

[5]

Table 3

Mass of bob/g	Average pendulum length/cm	First measurement of time for 10 oscillations/s	Second measurement of time for 10 oscillations/s	Average time for 10 oscillations/s	Period, T/s

[6]

Conclusions

What do your results suggest about how the length and the mass of a simple pendulum affect the period of the pendulum?

1 Length: [1]

....

....

....

2 Mass: [1]

....

....

....

Evaluation

Discuss how the experiment could be improved to give more reliable results.   [2]

....

....

....

....

....

....

Extension

Theory shows that:

$$g = \frac{40\,l}{T^2}$$

where *l* is the length of the pendulum, measured from the point of suspension to the centre of mass of the bob, in metres, and *T* is the period, in seconds. Calculate *g* using one set of your results.

g = ... m/s^2 [2]

1.2 Density

Aim

To measure the density of some liquids and solids.

Theory

By definition, the density of a substance is given by:

$$\text{density} = \frac{\text{mass}}{\text{volume}}$$

For a regular shaped solid the volume can be found by measuring its dimensions and the mass is determined by weighing. For an irregularly shaped solid the volume is found by immersion in a liquid.

Apparatus

- [ ] measuring cylinder
- [ ] ruler
- [ ] micrometer screw gauge
- [ ] scales
- [ ] solid blocks of different materials (A and B)
- [ ] length of wire (C)
- [ ] ball (D)
- [ ] irregularly shaped solid (E)
- [ ] water

Procedure

Regularly shaped solids

1 Select blocks A and B, which are made of two different materials.

2 Measure the dimensions of each block and record the values in Table 1.

3 Measure and record the mass of each block.

4 Select wire C; record its mass and dimensions in Table 2.

5 Select the ball D; record its mass and diameter in Table 2.

Liquid

1 Weigh an empty measuring cylinder and record the value in Table 3.

2 Pour some water into the measuring cylinder and reweigh it.

3 Record the new weight of the cylinder plus water.

4 Read and record the volume of water in the cylinder.

Irregularly shaped solid

1 Weigh and record the mass of object E in Table 4.

2 Put some water in a measuring cylinder and record its volume.

3 Place object E in the measuring cylinder so that it is covered with water.

4 Record the volume of water + E.

Method

The dimensions of the blocks A and B were measured with a .... to an

accuracy of ....   [1]

The diameter of the wire C was measured with a ....

to an accuracy of ....   [1]

Using two smooth vertical surfaces, explain how you could measure the diameter of
the ball D: [1]

....

....

....

....

....

....

The volume of object E was obtained by: [1]

....

....

....

Mass was measured with a balance of accuracy ....   [1]

Results and calculations

Complete the following equations and Tables 1, 2, 3 and 4 (including heading units).

Regularly shaped solids

1 Volume of a block = length × .... [1]

2 Volume of a wire = length × .... [1]

Note:

$$\text{volume of a sphere} = \frac{4\pi r^3}{3}$$

where r = radius of sphere.

Table 1

Object	Length/	Width/	Height/	Volume/	Mass/	Density/
A						
B						

[2]

Table 2

Object	Length/	First measurement of diameter/	Second measurement of diameter/	Average diameter/	Volume/	Mass/	Density/
C							
D							

[2]

Liquid

Table 3

Mass of empty cylinder/	Mass of cylinder + water/	Mass of water/	Volume of water/	Density of water/

[2]

Irregularly shaped solid

Table 4

Mass of E/	Volume of water/	Volume of water + E/	Volume of E/	Density of E/

[3]

Conclusions

Complete Table 5, and identify possible materials from which A, B, C, D and E are made from the values you obtained for their densities. Include the units in the heading for density.

Table 5

Object	Density/	Material
A		
B		
C		
D		
water		water
E		

[2]

Evaluation

Discuss how the experiment could be improved to give more reliable results. [1]

....

....

....

....

....

....

Extension

How could you determine whether a teaspoon is made of silver or steel?   [1]

....

....

....

....

....

....

1.3 Motion

Aim

To measure speed and acceleration.

Theory

Definitions:

$$\text{average speed} = \frac{\text{distance moved}}{\text{time taken}}$$

$$\text{acceleration} = \frac{\text{change of velocity}}{\text{time taken for the change}}$$

Apparatus

☐ tickertape timer
☐ trolley
☐ runway

Procedure

Distance/time

1 Familiarise yourself with the use of the tickertape timer.

2 With the timer switched on, pull a 1 m length of tape through the timer – first quickly, then slowly.

3 Cut the tape into ten-tick lengths and make a tape chart.

Velocity/time

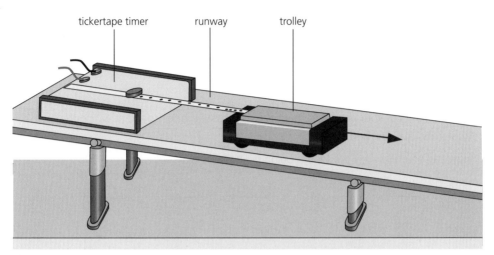

tickertape timer   runway   trolley

Figure 1

1 Set up a sloping runway, tickertape timer and trolley as shown in Figure 1.

2 Attach a length of tape to the trolley and release it at the top of the runway.

3 Ignore the region at the start where the dots are very close together, but beyond them cut the tape into ten-tick lengths and make a tape chart.

Method

Describe how a tickertape timer works; mention any difficulties encountered and precautions taken to achieve good results.   [2]

....

....

....

....

....

....

....

....

Results and calculations

Note that dots occur on the tape 50 times each second – that is, one dot every $\frac{1}{50}$ s (called a 'tick').

A 'ten-tick' corresponds to $10 \times \frac{1}{50}$ s $= \frac{1}{5}$ s

Distance/time

1   Label the axes of your chart and mark the regions where the speed at which the tape was pulled was fast and slow.   [3]

2   How can you tell when the tape is being pulled fast?   [1]

    ....

    ....

    ....

3   Find a region of the chart where the speed was constant and calculate that speed in cm/s.   [2]

    ....

    ....

    ....

Velocity/time

1   Label the axes of your chart.   [1]

2   Calculate the speed of the trolley, v_1 and v_2, for two adjacent tapes.   [4]

3 Use the two speeds to calculate the acceleration of the trolley in cm/s². [2]

4 Is the acceleration of the trolley constant? Justify your answer. [1]

....

....

....

Conclusions

Summarise the values you obtained in the experiment for speed and acceleration. [1]

....

....

....

Evaluation

Discuss how the experiment could be improved to give more reliable results. [1]

....

....

....

Extension

1 What is the acceleration of a body when it reaches its terminal velocity? [1]

....

....

....

2 What forces on a freely falling body are equal in magnitude when it reaches its
terminal velocity? [1]

....

....

....

1.4 Hooke's law

Aim

To investigate Hooke's law for a spring.

Theory

Hooke's law states that:

$$F = kx$$

where F is the stretching force, x is the extension of the spring and k is the spring constant. The law should hold if the spring is not permanently stretched.

Variables

Complete Table 1.

Table 1

Manipulated (independent)	Fixed	Responding (dependent)

[1]

Apparatus

☐ retort stand
☐ spring
☐ hanger with 100 g weights
☐ ruler
☐ adhesive/sticky tape

Procedure

Set up the apparatus as shown in Figure 1.

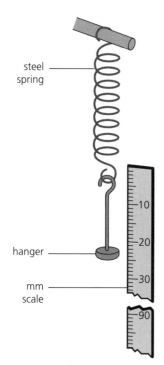

Safety!

Take care with masses and think where the hanging masses would fall if the spring snapped.

Wear eye protection when instructed.

Figure 1

1 Fix the ruler vertically next to the spring so that it can be used as a scale.

2 Record the position of the bottom of the unweighted spring on the scale, l_s, and repeat your measurement.

3 Measure the length of the hanger, l_o.

4 Hang an unweighted (100 g) hanger on the spring and record the scale position of the bottom of the hanger.

5 Add a 100 g mass to the hanger and again record the scale position of the bottom of the hanger.

6 Repeat step **5** with 200 g, 300 g, 400 g and 500 g masses on the hanger.

7 Plot a graph of the stretching force along the *x*-axis against the extension along the *y*-axis.

8 Calculate the gradient of the graph.

Method

Explain the method you used to measure the extension of the spring as accurately as possible.   [2]

....

....

....

....

....

....

....

....

....

....

Results and calculations

1 Complete the following.

   (a) Average position of bottom of unweighted spring on the scale, l_s =

   .... mm

   (b) Length of hanger, l_o = ... mm

2 Complete Table 2. Take the force exerted by gravity on a mass of 100 g to be 1 N.

   Note:

       extension of spring = scale reading of bottom of hanger − $(l_o + l_s)$

Table 2

Mass/g	Stretching force/N	Scale reading/mm	Extension/mm

[6]

3 Plot a graph of the stretching force along the *x*-axis against the extension along the *y*-axis.

[4]

Summary of results

Gradient of graph =   [2]

....

Conclusions

State whether or not the extension is proportional to the stretching force on the spring.   [1]

....

....

....

What do your results suggest about the validity of Hooke's law?   [1]

....

....

....

Evaluation

Discuss how the experiment could be improved to give more reliable results.   [2]

....

....

....

....

....

....

Extension

Calculate the value of the spring constant, k.

$$k = \frac{1}{\text{gradient of graph}}$$

$k =$ .... N/mm   [1]

1.5 Balancing a beam

Aim

To measure the moment of a force about a pivot and to show that there is no net moment on a body in equilibrium.

Theory

The moment of a force is a measure of its turning effect and is given by:

moment of a force = $F \times d$

where F is the turning force acting on a body and d is the perpendicular distance of the line of action of the force from the fulcrum.

For a body in equilibrium the law of moments states that the sum of the anticlockwise moments about any point equals the sum of the clockwise moments about the same point.

Variables

Complete Table 1.

Table 1

Manipulated (independent)	Fixed	Responding (dependent)

[1]

Apparatus

☐ retort stand
☐ half-metre ruler
☐ fulcrum (pivot)
☐ 3 hangers with sets of 10 g and 20 g masses
☐ scales
☐ blu-tack or adhesive/mounting putty

Procedure

Set up the apparatus as shown in Figure 1, with the fulcrum (nail) supported horizontally in a retort stand.

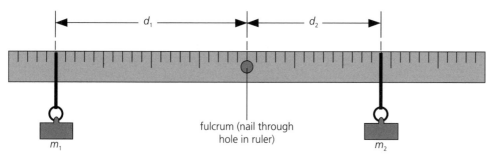

Figure 1

1 Balance the half-metre ruler at its centre, adding blu-tack to one side or the other until it is horizontal.

2 Hang a 30 g mass (m_1) from the ruler at a distance (d_1) of 20 cm from the fulcrum. Use a very small amount of blu-tack or tape to help hold it in place.

3 Hang a 40 g mass (m_2) on the opposite side of the fulcrum in such a position that the beam is balanced. Record the positions of m_1 and m_2 on the ruler in Table 2.

4 Move m_1 5 cm nearer to the fulcrum and adjust the position of m_2 until the beam is again balanced; record the new positions of the masses.

5 Repeat step **4**.

6 Change the masses m_1 and m_2 to 50 g and 60 g and repeat steps **2** to **5**.

7 Select masses of 30 g, 40 g and 50 g (M_1, M_2 and M_3) and balance the beam with two masses (at different positions) on one side of the fulcrum and one mass on the opposite side; record the position of each of the masses in Table 3.

Method

Mention equipment used, measurements made, precautions taken to achieve good results and any difficulties encountered in the experiment. [2]

....

....

....

....

....

....

....

....

....

....

Results and calculations

Complete the following tables. Take the force exerted on a mass of 10 g to be 0.1 N.

Table 2

m_1/g	F_1/N	Position on ruler/ cm	d_1/cm	$F_1 \times d_1$/ N cm	m_2/g	F_2/N	Position on ruler/ cm	d_2/cm	$F_2 \times d_2$/ N cm	Net moment/ N cm

[6]

Table 3

	Mass/g	F/N	Position on ruler/ cm	d/cm	$F \times d$/N cm	Anti-clockwise moment/N cm	Clockwise moment/N cm
M_1							
M_2							
M_3							

[3]

Conclusions

1 When the beam is in equilibrium, what do your results suggest about the values of the anticlockwise and clockwise moments? [2]

....

....

....

2 When the beam is in equilibrium, what do your results suggest about the net moment on the beam? [2]

....

....

....

Evaluation

Discuss how the experiment could be improved to give more reliable results. [2]

....

....

....

....

....

....

Extension

How could you use the apparatus to obtain the mass of an unknown object?   [2]

....

....

....

....

....

....

1.6 Centre of mass

Aim

To find the centre of mass of irregularly and regularly shaped laminae.

Theory

A body behaves as if its whole mass were concentrated at one point, called its centre of mass; the weight of the body can be considered to act at its centre of mass. When a body is suspended from a point, its centre of mass lies vertically below the point of suspension.

Variables

Complete Table 1.

Table 1

Manipulated (independent)	Fixed	Responding (dependent)

[1]

Apparatus

- ☐ retort stand
- ☐ nail
- ☐ regular and irregular cardboard laminae
- ☐ plumb line
- ☐ ruler

Procedure

Set up the apparatus as shown in Figure 1.

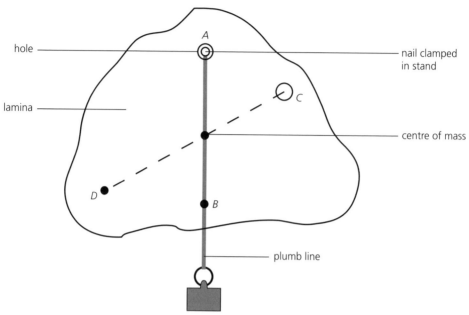

Figure 1

1. Make a hole (*A*) in the irregularly shaped lamina and suspend it from a nail clamped in the retort stand. Ensure that the lamina can swing freely.

2. With the lamina at rest, suspend a plumb line from the nail and mark its position on the lamina. Draw the line *AB* on the cardboard.

3. Make a second hole (*C*) in the cardboard and repeat step **2** with the lamina now suspended from *C*. Draw the line *CD*.

4. Make a third hole (*E*) in the cardboard and check that when the lamina is suspended from *E*, the plumb line passes through the intersection of the lines *AB* and *CD*.

5. Repeat steps **1** to **4** with a regularly shaped lamina.

Method

Mention measurements made, equipment used, precautions taken to achieve good results and any difficulties encountered. [2]

....

....

....

....

....

....

....

....

....

....

Results and calculations

Mark and label the position of the centre of mass on each of the cardboard lamina.   [8]

Conclusions

Complete the following paragraph.

When a body is .... from a point, its centre .... lies

.... below the point of suspension. By drawing in the vertical lines on a

lamina below .... different points of .... the place where

the two lines .... marks the position of the .... of mass.

The vertical line drawn from any other .... of suspension passes through

the centre of mass.   [2]

Evaluation

Discuss how the experiment could be improved to give more reliable results.   [2]

....

....

....

....

....

....

Extension

1 Locate and mark the centre of gravity in the following laminae:

   (a) rectangle   [1]

(b) circle [1]

(c) equilateral triangle [1]

2 Will a rectangle be more stable if it is resting on its short or long side? Explain your answer. [2]

....

....

....

....

....

....

1.7 Pressure

Aim

To measure the pressure of a gas using a water manometer.

Theory

The pressure due to a column of liquid is given by:

$$\text{pressure} = h \times \rho \times g$$

where h is the height of the liquid column, ρ is the density of the liquid and g is the strength of the Earth's gravitational field.

In a manometer:

$$\text{pressure of a gas} = \text{atmospheric pressure} + h\rho g$$

Variables

Complete Table 1.

Table 1

Manipulated (independent)	Fixed	Responding (dependent)

[1]

Apparatus

☐ Water manometer (U-tube should be at least 1 m long and be half-filled with water.)

Procedure

Atmospheric pressure

Atmospheric pressure can be measured with an aneroid or mercury barometer; the latter is becoming less used than formerly due to the toxic nature of mercury. In this experiment the use of a mercury barometer is considered theoretically and a representative value for atmospheric pressure of 76 cm Hg should be used for calculations.

Manometer

1 Blow into one arm of the manometer to change the air pressure on the liquid. Record in Table 2 the heights of the liquid in each arm of the manometer.

2 Repeat step **1** two times.

Method

Atmospheric pressure

Make a sketch of a mercury barometer.

Label some important features of a barometer in your sketch and indicate how a reading of atmospheric pressure is obtained.   [3]

Manometer

Make a sketch of the manometer indicating the liquid levels in the arms when there is:

1 equal pressure in each arm [1]

2 unequal pressure in the two arms. [2]

Results and calculations

Atmospheric pressure

Calculate the atmospheric pressure in Pa (N/m²) for a barometer reading of 76 cm Hg, taking the density of mercury to be 13 600 kg/m³ and $g = 10 \dfrac{N}{kg}$.

Atmospheric pressure = ... m Hg [1]

Atmospheric pressure = ... Pa [1]

Manometer

Complete the following equation and Table 2.

Density of water in manometer, ρ = ... $\dfrac{kg}{m^3}$ [1]

Density of water = $1.0 \dfrac{g}{cm^3}$

Table 2

Height of left hand column/m	Height of right hand column/m	Height difference, h/m	Pressure difference, $h\rho g$ / Pa	Gas pressure/ Pa

[6]

Conclusions

Summarise your results. [1]

....

....

....

....

....

....

Evaluation

Discuss how the experiment could be improved to give more reliable results. [1]

....

....

....

....

....

....

Extension

Explain if the reading on a barometer would change if the tube were narrower, or tilted.

1 Narrower   [1]

....

....

....

2 Tilted   [1]

....

....

....

2.1 Specific heat capacity

Aim

To measure the specific heat capacity of a liquid and a solid.

Theory

The heat, Q, required to raise the temperature of a mass, m, of a material by an amount ΔT is given by:

$$Q = m \times c \times \Delta T$$

where c is the specific heat capacity of the material.

Apparatus

☐ thermometer
☐ electric immersion heater (12 V, 50 W)
☐ calorimeter or can
☐ solid metal cylinder (with one central hole and one other hole)
☐ water
☐ scales
☐ timer

 Warning!
Hot liquids and solids – set in a safe position where they will not be accidentally knocked over; handle with caution to avoid burns.

Procedure

Liquid

1 Weigh an empty calorimeter.

2 Add 1 kg of water.

3 Record the temperature of the water, T_1, in Table 1.

4 Insert the immersion heater into the water.

5 Switch on the heater and start timing.

6 Stir the water and after 5 minutes switch off the heater.

7 Continue stirring the water and note the highest temperature reached, T_2.

Solid

1 Weigh the metal cylinder.

2 Place the immersion heater in the central hole of the cylinder and the thermometer in the other hole.

3 Record the temperature, T_1, of the cylinder in Table 2.

4 Switch on the immersion heater and start timing.

5 After 5 minutes turn off the heater.

6 When the temperature stops rising record the highest temperature, T_2, reached by the thermometer.

Method

Make a sketch of the apparatus on page 58, and mention below observations and measurements made, precautions taken to achieve good results and difficulties encountered.

[3]

....

....

....

....

....

....

Make a sketch of the apparatus below.

Results and calculations

Liquid

1 Complete the following equations and Table 1.

   (a) power of heater, P = ...

   (b) mass of water, m = ...

Table 1

Initial temperature, T_1/°C	Highest temperature, T_2/°C	Change in temperature, ΔT/°C	Heating time, t/s	Heat supplied, $Q = Pt$ / J

[4]

2 Rearranging the equation for the definition of specific heat capacity gives:

$$c = \frac{Q}{m \times \Delta T}$$

Calculate the specific heat capacity of water.

Specific heat capacity of water = ... J/(kg °C)   [2]

Solid

1 Complete the following equations and Table 2.

   (a) power of heater, P = ...

   (b) mass of metal cylinder, M = ...

Table 2

Initial temperature, T_1/°C	Highest temperature, T_2/°C	Change in temperature, ΔT/°C	Heating time, t/s	Heat supplied, $Q = Pt$ / J

[4]

2 Calculate the specific heat capacity of the metal cylinder.

Specific heat capacity of metal cylinder = ... J/(kg °C)   [2]

Conclusions

Summarise your results and compare with the expected values from tables. Suggest reasons for any differences.   [2]

....

....

....

....

....

....

Evaluation

Discuss how the experiment could be improved to give more reliable results. [1]

....

....

....

....

....

....

Extension

1 What is the thermal capacity of the water used in the first part of this experiment? [1]

....

2 What is the thermal capacity of the metal cylinder used in the second part of this experiment? [1]

....

2.2 Specific latent heat

Aim

To measure the specific latent heat of fusion of ice, and the specific latent heat of vaporisation of steam.

Theory

The heat, Q, required to change the mass, m, of a substance from solid to liquid without a change in temperature is given by:

$$Q = m \times l_f$$

where l_f is the specific latent heat of fusion.

Apparatus

- [ ] electric immersion heater (12 V, 50 W is suitable)
- [ ] funnel
- [ ] crushed ice
- [ ] beaker
- [ ] timer
- [ ] electronic scales
- [ ] insulating mats
- [ ] hot water

Procedure

Specific latent heat of fusion of ice

1 Set up the apparatus as shown in Figure 1; pack the ice closely around the immersion heater. Do not switch on the immersion heater yet.

2 When the ice has started melting, empty the beaker, and collect melted ice for 4 minutes.

3 Measure and record the mass, m_1, of water collected.

4 Empty the beaker and turn on the immersion heater for 4 minutes.

5 Measure and record the new mass, m_2, of water collected.

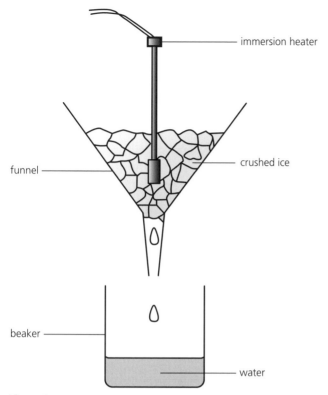

funnel

immersion heater

crushed ice

beaker

water

Figure 1

Specific latent heat of vaporisation of steam

Warning!
Take care when dealing with beakers of boiling water.

1 Put about 200 g of hot water in a beaker.

2 Place the immersion heater in the beaker so that the coil is covered by water and bring the water to the boil.

3 Turn off the heater, remove it from the beaker and set it on an insulating mat.

4 Weigh the beaker of water on some electronic scales (protected by another insulating mat) and record the mass, m_3, of the (mat + beaker + water).

5 Remove the beaker from the scales, replace the immersion heater in the water and switch it on.

6 When the water begins to boil again, start the timer.

7 After 5 minutes turn the heater off and remove it from the water, ensuring any water drops back into the beaker.

8 Reweigh and record the mass, m_4, of the (mat + beaker + water).

63

Method

1 Explain why:
   (a) the ice should be melting before measurements are started. [1]

   ....

   ....

   ....

   ....

   (b) the mass of ice melting without the heater switched on, m_1, is first collected. [1]

   ....

   ....

   ....

   ....

2 **(a)** How can you tell when the water is boiling? [1]

   ....

   ....

   (b) What is the temperature of the water when it is boiling? [1]

   ....

   ....

Results and calculations

Specific latent heat of fusion of ice

1 Complete the following.
   (a) power of immersion heater, P = ...
   (b) heat supplied by immersion heater in 4 minutes,
      $Q = P \times$ time in seconds = ... [1]
   (c) mass of ice melted by heat from surroundings, m_1 = ... [1]
   (d) mass of ice melted by heater and surroundings, m_2 = ... [1]
   (e) mass of ice melted by heater, $m = (m_2 - m_1)$ = ... [1]

2 Rearranging the equation for specific latent heat gives:

$$l_f = \frac{Q}{m}$$

Calculate the specific latent heat of fusion of ice.

Specific latent heat of fusion of ice = ... J/kg [2]

Specific latent heat of vaporisation of steam

1 Complete the following.
(a) power of immersion heater, P = ...
(b) heat supplied by immersion heater in 5 minutes,

$Q = P \times$ time in seconds = ... [1]
(c) mass of (mat + beaker + water), m_3 = ... [1]
(d) mass of (mat + beaker + water after boiling for 5 minutes),

m_4 = ... [1]
(e) mass of water changed to steam, $m = (m_3 - m_4)$ = ... [1]

2 Rearranging the equation for specific latent heat gives:

$$l_v = \frac{Q}{m}$$

Calculate the specific latent heat of vaporisation of steam (l_v).

Specific latent heat of vaporisation of steam = ... J/kg [2]

Conclusions

Summarise your results and compare them with the expected values from tables. Suggest reasons for any differences. [2]

....

....

....

....

....

....

Evaluation

Discuss how the experiment could be improved to give more reliable results. [1]

....

....

....

....

....

Extension

Explain how the energy of the molecules in a solid changes when melting occurs. [1]

....

....

....

2.3 Conduction and radiation

Aim

To demonstrate the properties of good conductors and good radiators of heat.

Apparatus

- ☐ selection of rods of different materials having the same dimensions
- ☐ wax
- ☐ Bunsen burner
- ☐ tripod
- ☐ timer
- ☐ 2 identical thermometers (one with bulb painted dull black)
- ☐ beaker of hot water
- ☐ 2 retort stands
- ☐ card

 Warning!
Hot liquids and solids – set in a safe position where they will not be accidentally knocked over; handle with caution to avoid burns.

Procedure

Conduction

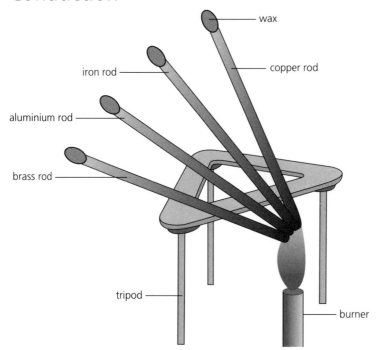

wax

copper rod

iron rod

aluminium rod

brass rod

tripod

burner

1 Melt a small blob of wax onto one end of each rod.

2 Rest the rods on a tripod and arrange them in a fan shape such that the unwaxed ends of each rod are close together and the waxed ends are separated. Place a card under the wax to catch the drips!

3 Start the timer and heat the unwaxed end of the rods evenly and gently with a Bunsen burner.

4 Record the time at which the wax starts to drip from each of the rods.

Radiation

1 Select one thermometer with an unpainted bulb and one with a bulb painted black.

2 Record the room temperature.

3 Place the thermometers in a beaker of hot water and wait until they reach the same steady temperature; record this temperature.

4 Remove the thermometers from the water at the same moment and start the timer.

5 Clamp each thermometer in a retort stand (at least 20 cm away from each other and from the hot water, and also away from any draughts).

6 Record the temperature of each thermometer every 30 seconds.

7 Plot a graph to show how the temperature reading on each thermometer varied with time.

Method

Conduction

How is heat transferred along the metal rods? [1]

....

Radiation

1 Explain why the two thermometers should have the same temperature when removed from the hot water. [1]

....

....

....

....

....

....

....

2 Why should the thermometers be shielded from a draught? [1]

....

....

....

....

....

....

Results and calculations

Conduction

Complete Table 1, including the units in the header.

Table 1

Material	Time taken by wax to melt

[2]

Radiation

1 Complete the following.

Room temperature = ... °C

Table 2

Time/s	Temperature of thermometer with black bulb/°C	Temperature of thermometer with shiny bulb/°C

[4]

2 Plot a graph of temperature on the *y*-axis and time on the *x*-axis for each thermometer [4]

Conclusions

1 (a) How can you tell which material is the best conductor of heat? [1]

....

(b) List the materials in order of conductivity from best to worst. [1]

....

....

2 (a) Which thermometer cools down fastest? [1]

....

(b) A dull black surface emits radiation .... a shiny surface. [1]

Evaluation

1 Suggest how the conduction experiment could be improved to give more reliable results. [1]

....

....

....

....

....

....

2 Suggest how the radiation experiment could be improved to give more reliable results. [1]

....

....

....

....

....

....

Extension

Discuss whether a central heating radiator should be painted black or white. [1]

....

....

....

3 Properties of waves

3.1 Law of reflection

Aim

To verify the law of reflection and identify the properties of an image in a plane mirror.

Theory

The law of reflection states that the angle of incidence equals the angle of reflection:

$$i = r$$

where i is the angle between the incident ray and the normal to the reflecting surface and r is the angle between the reflected ray and the normal to the reflecting surface.

Apparatus

- [ ] lamp
- [ ] single slit
- [ ] plane mirror
- [ ] pins
- [ ] protractor
- [ ] blu-tack or adhesive/mounting putty

Procedure

Take care, the lamp can get hot!

1 In Figure 2, use a protractor to draw in lines from O at 15°, 30°, 45°, 60° and 75° to the normal ON (as indicated in Figure 1).

2 Place a plane mirror vertically on the line AOB; blu-tack may be helpful to hold it in position.

3 Align the lamp and single slit so that a beam of light is incident on the mirror along the 15° line; mark the position of the reflected ray.

4 Repeat step **3** for the other angles of incidence.

5 Remove the mirror and measure the angle of reflection for each ray.

6 Record your results in Table 1.

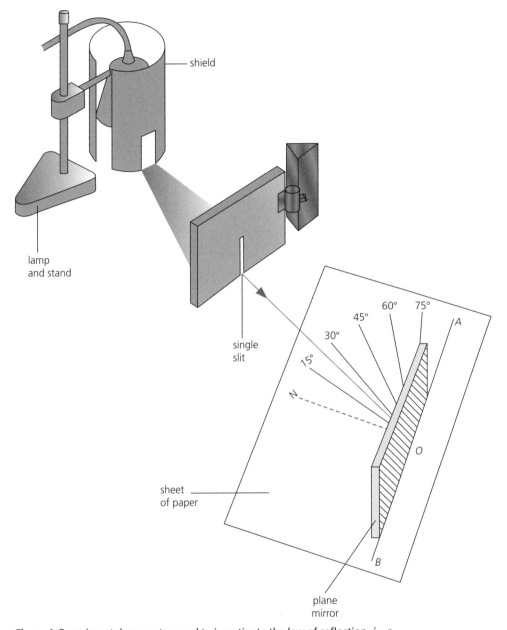

Figure 1 Experimental apparatus used to investigate the law of reflection, $i = r$

7 Replace the mirror on line *AOB*.

8 Mark a point about 3 cm from the mirror on the 30° incidence line; set a pin vertically on this point, P_O.

9 Locate the image of the pin in the mirror by looking along the 30° reflection line; mark the apparent position, P_I, of the image behind the mirror with a second pin.

10 Measure and record the positions of P_O and P_I.

75

Method

Complete the following sentences:

1 It is important to align the reflecting surface of the mirror exactly along line *AOB* to: [1]

....

2 The accuracy of measurements taken with a protractor is: [1]

....

Results and calculations

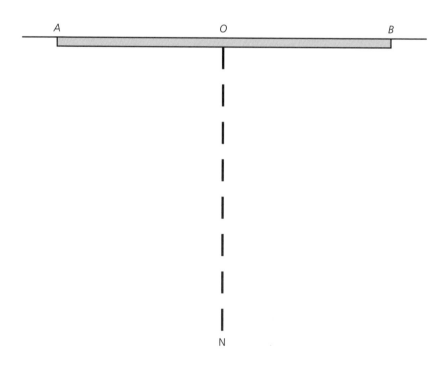

Figure 2

[3]

Complete the following table and equations:

Table 1

Angle of incidence, $i/°$	Angle of reflection, $r/°$

[5]

Along a line joining P_O and P_I the:

perpendicular distance of P_O from mirror = ... [1]

perpendicular distance of P_I from mirror = ... [1]

Conclusions

1 My results .... the law of reflection, within experimental

.... [1]

2 The image in a plane mirror is formed at a position that is: [2]

....

....

....

....

3 The image formed in a plane mirror has the following characteristics: [2]

....

....

....

....

Evaluation

Discuss how the experiment could be improved to give more reliable results. [1]

....

....

....

....

....

....

Extension

1 Explain what is meant by lateral inversion. [1]

....

....

....

....

....

2 How could you test if the image in a plane mirror is laterally inverted? [1]

....

....

....

....

....

3.2 Refraction of light

Aim

To determine the refractive index of glass and to observe the path of light rays passing through a glass block.

Theory

The refractive index, n, of a medium is given by:

$$n = \frac{\sin i}{\sin r}$$

where i is the angle between the incident ray in air and the normal and r is the angle between the refracted ray and the normal in the medium.

Variables

Complete Table 1.

Table 1

Manipulated (independent)	Fixed	Responding (dependent)

[1]

Apparatus

- ☐ lamp
- ☐ single slit
- ☐ glass block with lower surface painted white
- ☐ protractor

Procedure

 Warning!
Take care, the lamp can get hot!

1 Place the glass block with the white painted surface on the paper and its long side along line *AOB* in Figure 1 below. Draw the outline of your block onto the paper.

2 Mark the normal to the block at *O*.

3 Align the lamp and single slit so that a beam of light is incident on the block at *O* at an angle of incidence of about 30°.

4   Draw in the incident ray, refracted ray and emergent ray; measure the exact angle of each to the surface normal with a protractor and record your results in Table 2.

5   Repeat steps **3** and **4** with an angle of incidence of 60° and 0°.

6   Move the lamp, slit and glass block to Figure 2. Set the glass block with its short side along the line *AOC* and draw the outline of your block on the paper.

7   Repeat steps **2** to **5**, recording your results in Table 3.

Method

Complete the following sentences.

1   The angle in degrees between the normal and the surface (*AOB*) of the glass block is: [1]

   ....

2   The paths of the refracted and emergent rays were determined by marking: [1]

   ....

Results and calculations

1   Complete Figure 1 and Table 2.

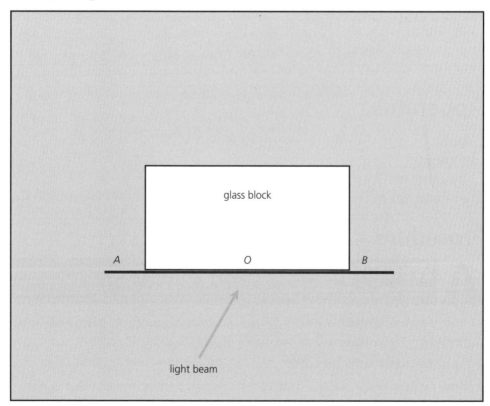

Figure 1

Table 2 Light beam incident on *AB*

Angle of incidence, $i/°$	Angle of refraction, $r/°$	Angle of emergent ray, $\theta/°$	sin i	sin r	$n = \dfrac{\sin i}{\sin r}$

[5]

2   Complete Figure 2 and Table 3.

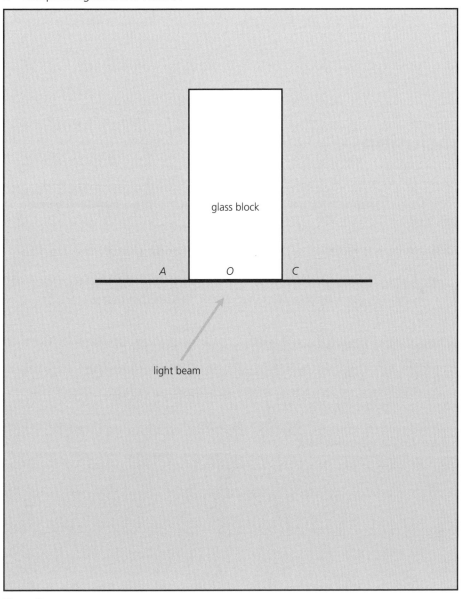

Figure 2

Table 3 Light beam incident on *AC*

Angle of incidence, *i*/°	Angle of refraction, *r*/°	Angle of emergent ray, θ/°	sin *i*	sin *r*	$n = \dfrac{\sin i}{\sin r}$

[5]

3 Calculate an average value for the refractive index of glass. [2]

....

....

....

Conclusions

1 The average value for the refractive index of the glass block is .... [1]

2 Complete the following sentences about the path of light rays travelling through the glass block.

(a) A light ray is refracted .... the normal when it enters the glass

block and .... the normal when it leaves the block. [1]

(b) A ray incident normally on a glass block is not refracted but passes

.... the block. [1]

(c) When a light ray strikes the glass/air boundary at a large angle, total internal reflection of the light occurs. If a light ray does not undergo

.... in the block, the ray emerges

.... to the incident ray, since *i* = ... within the accuracy of the experiment. [1]

Evaluation

Discuss how the experiment could be improved to give more reliable results. [1]

....

....

....

....

Extension

1 Explain what is meant by the **critical angle**, c. [1]

....

....

....

....

....

2 In the above experiment, the critical angle is given by the expression:

$$\sin c = \frac{1}{n}$$

From your results determine the value of c for the glass block. [1]

....

....

....

3.3 Lenses

Aim

To determine the focal length and the linear magnification of a converging lens.

Theory

Parallel rays from a distant object converge towards the principal focus of a converging lens.

The linear magnification, *m*, of an image is given by:

$$m = \frac{\text{height of image}}{\text{height of object}}$$

Apparatus

☐ small torch and stand
☐ converging lens
☐ card
☐ paper
☐ metre rule
☐ blu-tack or adhesive/mounting putty

Variables

Complete Table 1.

Table 1

Manipulated (independent)	Fixed	Responding (dependent)

[1]

Procedure

Focal length of a lens

1 Hold the lens up to a distant window and form a sharp image of the window on the wall or a piece of card.

2 Measure and record the distance between the lens and the card, the image distance, *v*.

3 Repeat steps **1** and **2** and obtain an average value for the image distance, *v*, which is equal to the focal length, *f*, of the lens.

Magnification

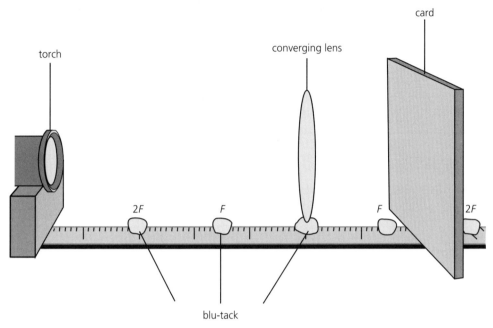

Figure 1

1 Set up the apparatus as shown in Figure 1. Use some blu-tack to hold the lens vertically upright at the 50 cm mark of a metre rule resting horizontally on the bench.

2 Use a little blu-tack to mark the position on the ruler of the principal focus, *F*, on each side of the lens. (The point *F* is a distance *f* from the centre of the lens.) Also mark the 2*F* position each side of the lens (which is 2 × *f* from the centre of the lens).

3 Using the torch as the object, set it beyond the 2*F* position facing the centre of the lens.

4 Measure and record the distance of the object from the lens, *u*.

5 Locate a sharp image of the object on a piece of card on the opposite side of the lens.

6 Measure and record the distance of the image from the lens, *v*.

7 Measure and record the height of the image and whether it is inverted or not.

8 Move the torch nearer to the lens, first to 2*F*, then to between 2*F* and *F*, and repeat steps **4** to **7** for each position.

9 Move the torch to a position between *F* and the lens; it will not be possible to form an image on the card. Reduce the brightness of the torch (by placing a thin piece of paper in front of it) and look back through the lens towards the torch. Estimate and record the distance of the image from the lens and its height; record whether the image is upright or inverted.

10 Record the height of the object.

Method

Complete the following sentences.

1 We found the height of the image by: [1]

....

....

....

....

....

2 We determined if the image was inverted or not by: [1]

....

....

....

Results and calculations

Complete the equations below and Table 2.

Focal length of lens

Object distance, u = infinity (distant window)

Image distance, v_1 = ..., v_2 = ...

Average image distance, v = ... [1]

Focal length, f, of lens = ...

Magnification

Height of object = ... cm [1]

Table 2

Torch position	Object distance, u/cm	Image distance, v/cm	Height of image/ cm	Linear magnification	Upright or inverted
beyond 2F					
at 2F					
between 2F and F					
between F and lens					

[8]

Conclusions

1 The focal length of the lens = ... cm   [1]

2 Summarise how the image distance, magnification and uprightness of the image varies with the object distance.   [2]

....

....

....

....

....

....

....

....

....

....

Evaluation

Discuss how the experiment could be improved to give more reliable results. [1]

....

....

....

....

....

Extension

1 Explain the difference between a real and a virtual image. [1]

....

....

....

....

....

....

2 Draw a ray diagram to show where the image is formed when the object lies between *F* and the lens. [2]

3.4 Speed of sound

Aim

To measure the speed of sound in air.

Theory

The speed of sound in air, v, is given by:

$$v = \frac{d}{t}$$

where d is the distance the sound travels in air in time, t.

Variables

Complete Table 1.

Table 1

Manipulated (independent)	Fixed	Responding (dependent)

[1]

Apparatus

- ☐ digital timer with millisecond accuracy
- ☐ 2 microphones
- ☐ small hammer
- ☐ metal plate
- ☐ metre rule

Procedure

Set up the apparatus as shown in Figure 1, with the microphones about 1 metre apart.

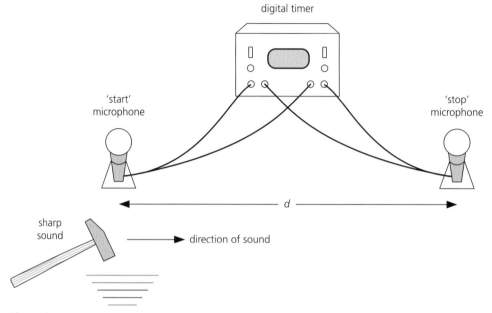

Figure 1

1   Measure and record the distance, d, between the centres of the 'start' and 'stop' microphones.

2   Switch on the timer so that it is ready to record.

3   Tap the hammer sharply on a metal plate placed close to the 'start' microphone; the timer should start.

4   The timer should stop when the sound reaches the 'stop' microphone.

5   Record the time, t_1, displayed on the timer.

6   Reset the timer and repeat steps **3** to **5**; record the time, t_2.

7   Move the microphones 10 cm closer to each other and repeat steps **1** to **6**.

8   Repeat step **7** three more times.

9   Plot a graph to show how the time taken for the sound to travel to the second microphone varies with its distance.

10 Calculate the gradient of the graph.

Method

The distance *d* was measured with .... and had an accuracy of about

....

Distance, *d*, was difficult to determine exactly because:

....

....

....

To ensure sounds from neighbouring experiments did not trigger our timer we: [2]

....

....

....

Results and calculations

Complete Table 2, the graph and the following equations.

Table 2

Distance, d/cm	First time measurement, t_1/ms	Second time measurement, t_2/ms	Average time, t/ms

[5]

1 Plot a graph of the average time, *t*, along the *x*-axis against the distance, *d*, along the *y*-axis.

[4]

2 Summary of results:

   (a) Gradient of graph   = ... cm/ms   [2]

   (b) Speed of sound in air = ... cm/ms   [1]

                     = ... m/s   [1]

Conclusions

State the value you obtained for the speed of sound in air. Compare your value with the expected value; suggest reasons for any difference.   [2]

....

....

....

....

....

Evaluation

Discuss how the experiment could be improved to give more reliable results. [1]

....

....

....

....

....

....

Extension

A sharp sound takes 50 μs to travel down an iron bar 30 cm long. Calculate the speed of sound in iron.

Speed of sound in iron = ... $\frac{m}{s}$ [1]

4.1 Electric charges and currents

Aim

To investigate the forces between electric charges; to measure currents in series and parallel circuits.

Apparatus

- [ ] 2 × 1.5 V cells
- [ ] 2 × 1.25 V lamps
- [ ] 0–1 A ammeter
- [ ] switch
- [ ] circuit board
- [ ] connecting wire
- [ ] polythene rods
- [ ] cellulose acetate strips
- [ ] cloth
- [ ] thread
- [ ] paper stirrup
- [ ] retort stand
- [ ] aluminium foil

Procedure

Positive and negative charges

1 Rub a polythene rod with a cloth.

2 Support the rod horizontally in a paper stirrup suspended from a retort stand; the rod should be able to swing freely.

3 Rub a second polythene rod and bring it close to the suspended rod; record whether the rods are attracted or repelled in Table 1.

4 Rub a strip of cellulose acetate with the cloth and bring it near to the suspended polythene rod; again record whether the rods are attracted or repelled.

Electric currents

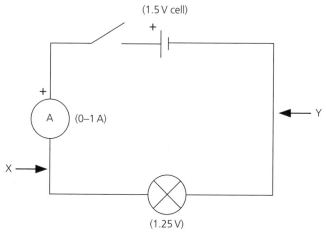

Figure 1

1 (a) Connect up the circuit of Figure 1 making sure that the + terminal of the cell goes to the + terminal (red) of the ammeter. When the switch is closed and the lamp is on, record the reading of the current through the ammeter in Table 2.

(b) Disconnect the ammeter and reinsert it in the circuit at position Y. When the circuit is complete, record the current through the ammeter again.

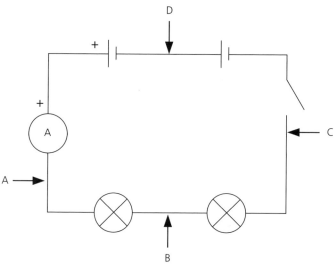

Figure 2

2 (a) Connect two cells and two lamps in *series* with the ammeter as shown in Figure 2. The + terminal of one cell should be connected to the – terminal of the other. When the switch is closed and both lamps are on, record the current reading through the ammeter in Table 2.

(b) Disconnect the ammeter and reinsert it in the circuit at position B. When the circuit is complete, record the value of the current through the ammeter.

(c) Repeat step **2(b)** with the ammeter inserted into positions C and then D in the circuit.

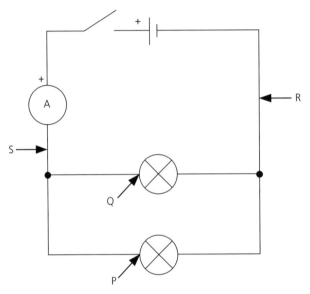

Figure 3

3 (a) Connect the two lamps in *parallel* with one cell as shown in Figure 3. When the switch is closed and both lamps are on, record the current passing through the ammeter in Table 2.

(b) Disconnect the ammeter and reinsert it in the circuit next to the lamp at position P. When the circuit is complete and both lamps are on, record the value of the current through the ammeter.

(c) Repeat step **3(b)** with the ammeter inserted into positions Q and then R in the circuit.

Method

Mention any difficulties encountered or precautions taken in performing the experiments. [2]

....

....

....

....

....

....

Results

Positive and negative charges

Complete Table 1 and the following sentences.

Table 1

Material of charged rod	Material of charged rod	Attracted or repelled

[2]

1 Like charges ....

2 Unlike charges ....

Electric currents

Complete Table 2.

Table 2

Ammeter position	Current/A
X	
Y	
A	
B	
C	
D	
S	
P	
Q	
R	

[10]

Conclusions

1 Complete the following sentence.

Like charges ...., unlike charges ....   [1]

2 Complete the following sentences.

(a) The current is .... at all points in a series circuit.   [1]

(b) The sum of the currents in the branches of a parallel circuit ....

the current entering .... the parallel section.   [1]

Evaluation

Discuss how the experiment could be improved to give more reliable results. [1]

....

....

....

....

Extension

1 Describe how charging occurs by electrostatic induction. [1]

....

....

....

....

....

....

2 Explain what happens and why, when a charged rod is brought close to some small pieces of aluminium foil on the bench. [1]

....

....

....

4.2 Resistance

Aim

To measure the resistance of a wire and investigate its dependence on length and diameter.

Theory

The resistance, R, of a wire is given by:

$$R = \frac{V}{I}$$

where V is the p.d. across the wire and I is the current flowing through it.

Apparatus

- ☐ 4.5 V battery (three 1.5 V cells connected in series can be used)
- ☐ ammeter (0–1 A)
- ☐ voltmeter (0–5 V)
- ☐ 0–25 Ω rheostat
- ☐ constantan wire
- ☐ micrometer screw gauge
- ☐ metre rule
- ☐ wires and connectors
- ☐ insulated circuit board with mounting clamps

Procedure

 Warning!
The constantan wire may become hot when current flows in it.

1   Set up the circuit shown in Figure 1 where the unknown resistance, R, is a 1 m length of constantan wire held above the circuit board in two vertical clamps.

2   Set the rheostat at its maximum resistance.

3   Record the current, I, in the circuit and the p.d., V, across the unknown resistance, R, in Table 1.

4   Reduce the resistance of the rheostat and record the new values of I and V.

5   Repeat step **4** until you have six different readings of I and V.

6   Plot a graph of V along the x-axis and I along the y-axis.

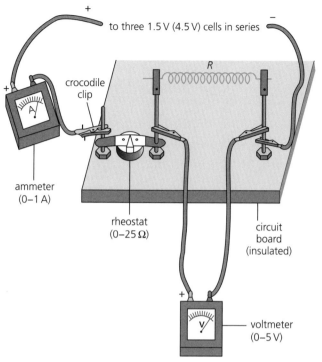

to three 1.5 V (4.5 V) cells in series

R

crocodile clip

ammeter (0–1 A)

rheostat (0–25 Ω)

circuit board (insulated)

voltmeter (0–5 V)

Figure 1

7 Reduce the length of constantan wire in the circuit to 50 cm; for a mid-range setting of the rheostat, record the current in the circuit and the p.d. across the wire in Table 2. Measure the diameter of the wire and record the value.

8 Replace the constantan wire in the circuit with one of a different diameter, again 1 m long. Measure the diameter of the wire and record the value in Table 2. For a mid-range setting of the rheostat, record the current in the circuit and the p.d. across the wire.

9 Repeat step **7**.

Method

Draw a circuit diagram of the experimental arrangement. [2]

Results and calculations

1 Complete Table 1.

Table 1

Current, I/A	p.d., V/V	Resistance, R/Ω

[4]

2 Plot a graph to show how the p.d., V, varies with the current, I. [3]

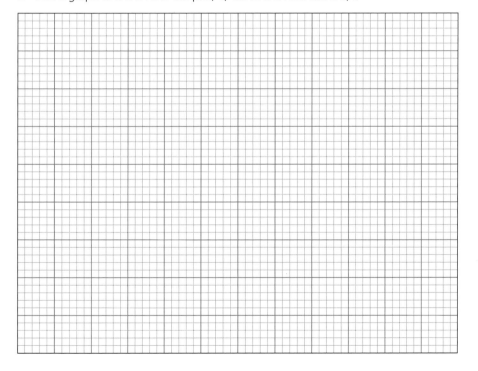

3 Find the gradient of your graph.

Gradient of graph = ... A/V [1]

Average resistance = 1/gradient of graph = ... Ω [1]

4 Complete Table 2.

Table 2

Length of constantan wire/cm	Diameter of wire/mm	Current, I/A	p.d., V/V	Resistance, R/Ω
100				
50				
100				
50				

[3]

Conclusions

1 State how the resistance of the wire changes when the current through it increases. [1]

....

....

....

2 State how the resistance of the wire varies with the length and diameter of the wire. [2]

....

....

....

....

....

....

Evaluation

Discuss how the experiment could be improved to give more reliable results. [1]

....

....

....

....

....

....

Extension

The resistance of a filament lamp increases when the current flowing through it increases.

1 Explain why. [1]

....

....

....

2 Sketch the *I*/*V* curve for a filament lamp. [1]

4.3 Potential divider

Aim

To investigate the action of a variable potential divider.

Theory

In a potential divider, the ratio of the voltages V_1 and V_2 across resistances R_1 and R_2 is given by:

$$\frac{V_1}{V_2} = \frac{R_1}{R_2}$$

Apparatus

☐ 6V battery (four 1.5V cells connected in series can be used)
☐ ammeter (0–1 mA)
☐ 2 voltmeters (0–10V)
☐ 10 kΩ resistor
☐ thermistor (TH7)
☐ matches
☐ wires and connectors

Procedure

Potential divider

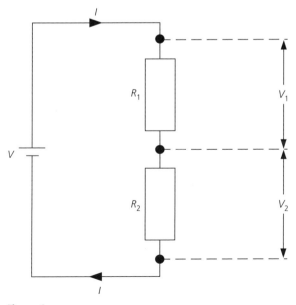

Figure 1

1   Set up the circuit shown in Figure 1 with R_1 as the 10 kΩ resistor and R_2 as a thermistor.

2   Insert the ammeter into the circuit to measure the current, I.

3   Connect a voltmeter across each of R_1 and R_2 to measure V_1 and V_2.

4   Record the values of I, V_1 and V_2 in Table 1.

5   Warm the thermistor with a match and record the new values of I, V_1 and V_2.

6   As the thermistor cools, record a third set of values for I, V_1 and V_2.

Method

Mention measurements made, difficulties encountered and precautions taken to achieve good results.   [2]

....

....

....

....

....

....

....

....

Results and calculations

1   Complete Table 1.

Table 1

I/mA	V_1/V	V_2/V	V_1/V_2	R_2/Ω	R_1/R_2

[4]

2   When the temperature of the thermistor rises, state if an increase or decrease occurs in:
    (a) I [1]

....

(b) V_1 [1]

....

(c) V_2 [1]

....

(d) R_2 [1]

....

3 Explain how the potential divider circuit could be used to monitor temperature. [1]

....

....

....

Conclusions

Summarise your results; are they in agreement with the potential divider equation? [2]

....

....

....

....

....

Evaluation

Discuss how the experiment could be improved to give more reliable results. [1]

....

....

....

Extension

High temperature alarm

Draw a circuit diagram that could be used for a high temperature alarm; include a thermistor, resistor, relay and bell. [3]

Control system

A control system is required to turn on an air conditioner when the temperature reaches a certain value when it is dark. Design a control system for this purpose using a temperature sensor, a light sensor, a NOT gate and an AND gate. [3]

4.4 Magnetism

Aim

To investigate the magnetic field lines around a bar magnet and between magnetic poles.

Theory

Unlike magnetic poles attract, like magnetic poles repel.

A magnetic field can be represented by lines of force; the direction of the field at any point is the direction of the force exerted on the north pole of a magnet in the field.

Apparatus

- ☐ 2 bar magnets
- ☐ plotting compass
- ☐ iron filings in a shaker
- ☐ paper

Procedure

Field lines around a bar magnet

1 Lay a bar magnet in the space indicated below (in the results section) and draw its outline.

2 Place a plotting compass near the north pole of the bar magnet (see point *A* in Figure 1).

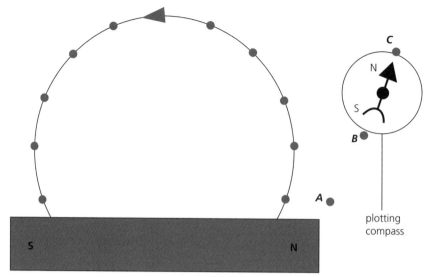

Figure 1

3   Mark the positions of the south and north poles of the compass needle (*A*, *B*) on the paper.

4   Move the compass so that the south pole of the compass needle is at the point (*B*) where the north pole was previously and mark the new position of the north pole of the compass needle (*C*).

5   Continue step **4** until the compass is near the south pole of the bar magnet.

6   Join up the points to give a field line.

7   Plot other field lines by repeating the steps **2** to **6** with the compass at different starting points.

Field lines between magnetic poles

 Safety!
Wear eye protection

1   Align two magnets with two like poles opposite each other, about 5 cm apart.

2   Place a piece of paper over the magnets.

3   Sprinkle some iron filings over the paper evenly and thinly; tap the paper gently so that the iron filings line up along magnetic field lines.

4   Sketch the appearance of the field lines below.

5   Repeat steps **1** to **4** with two unlike poles facing each other.

Method

1 Explain how you determined which was the north pole of the bar magnet. [1]

....

....

....

....

....

2 In which direction does the north pole of a compass needle point when it is placed in a magnetic field? [1]

....

....

....

3 Explain why the iron filings line up along magnetic field lines. [1]

....

....

....

....

....

Results

Field lines around a bar magnet

Plot the field lines around a bar magnet in the space below.   [7]

Field lines between magnetic poles

1 Sketch the field lines between two like poles. [3]

2 Sketch the field lines between two unlike poles. [3]

Conclusions

Complete the following sentences.

1 The magnetic field around a bar magnet is .... near the ends/poles, as

   is shown by the .... of magnetic field lines in this region.   [1]

2 Magnetic field lines are directed from the .... pole of a magnet to the

   .... pole.   [1]

Evaluation

Discuss how the experiments could be improved to give more reliable results.   [1]

....

....

....

....

....

Extension

Suggest one method by which a steel bar can be magnetised.   [1]

....

....

....

4.5 Electromagnetism

Aim

To construct and test an electromagnet, and to investigate Faraday's and Lenz's laws of electromagnetic induction.

Theory

- The **right hand-grip rule** states that if the fingers of the right hand grip the coil of an electromagnet in the direction of the current flow, the thumb points to the north pole produced.
- **Faraday's law** states that the size of an induced p.d. is directly proportional to the rate at which the conductor cuts magnetic field lines.
- **Lenz's law** states that the direction of the induced current is such as to oppose the change causing it.

Apparatus

- ☐ 3 m of PVC-covered copper wire (SWG 26)
- ☐ 5 cm long iron nail
- ☐ retort stand
- ☐ paper clips
- ☐ ammeter (0–2 A)
- ☐ rheostat (0–15 Ω)
- ☐ 3 V battery
- ☐ plotting compass
- ☐ bar magnet
- ☐ 600 turn coil
- ☐ sensitive centre-zero meter
- ☐ wires and connectors

Procedure

Electromagnet

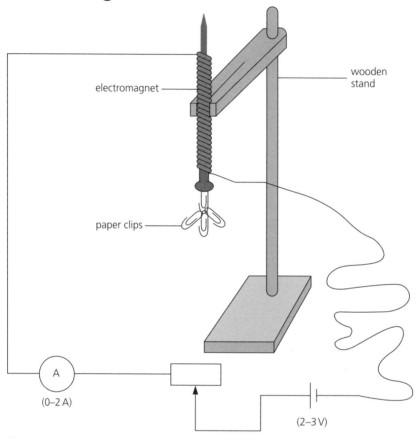

electromagnet

wooden
stand

paper clips

A

(0–2 A)

(2–3 V)

Figure 1

Safety!
Only switch on for a few seconds.

1 Leave about 25 cm at the end of the wire (for connecting to the circuit) and then wind about 50 cm of wire in a single layer onto the nail. Keep the turns close together, always wind in the same direction; keep approximate count of the number of turns of wire.

2 Connect up the circuit shown in Figure 1 with the rheostat set at maximum resistance.

3 In Table 1, record the number of paper clips the electromagnet can support for a range of currents between 0.2 and 2 A, including 1 A. For the 1 A current, also record the number of paper clips in Table 2.

4 Wind a second layer of wire back along the nail, winding in the same direction as the first layer.

5 In Table 2, record the number of paper clips now supported by a current of 1 A.

6 Use a plotting compass to determine the polarity of the coil when the current flows from the top to the bottom of the coil.

Electromagnetic induction

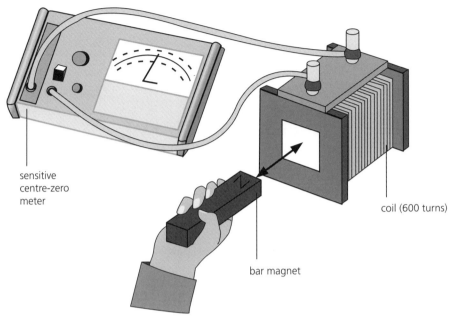

sensitive
centre-zero
meter

coil (600 turns)

bar magnet

Figure 2

1 Connect the 600-turn coil directly to a sensitive centre-zero meter as shown in Figure 2.

2 Identify the north pole of the bar magnet with the plotting compass.

3 In Table 3, record the direction and value of the maximum deflection of the meter when the north pole of the bar magnet is moved *quickly towards* the coil along the line of its axis.

4 Record the direction and value of the maximum deflection of the meter when the north pole of the bar magnet is moved *slowly towards* the coil.

5 Repeat steps **3** and **4** with the north pole of the magnet moving *away* from the coil.

6 In Table 4, record the direction and value of the maximum deflection of the meter when the coil is moved *quickly towards* the north pole of the magnet.

7 Record the direction and value of the maximum deflection of the meter when the coil is moved *quickly away from* the north pole of the magnet.

Method

1 What advantage does the electromagnet gain by having an iron core?   [1]

....

....

....

2 Why is a centre-zero meter used for studying electromagnetic induction? [1]

....

....

....

Results and calculations

Electromagnet

1 Complete Tables 1 and 2.

Table 1

Current, I/A	Number of paper clips supported

[3]

Table 2 Current in coils = 1 A

Number of turns on coil (approx)	Number of paper clips supported

[1]

2 Complete the following sentence. Check your answer using the right hand-grip rule. [1]

The top of the coil is a .... pole when current flows down the coil.

Electromagnetic induction

Complete Tables 3 and 4.

Table 3

Direction of movement of north pole	Speed of movement of magnet	Maximum current, I/A	Direction of current	Polarity of coil end facing magnet

[3]

Table 4

Direction of movement of coil	Speed of movement of coil	Maximum current, I/A	Direction of current	Polarity of coil end facing magnet

[2]

Conclusions

1 Suggest how the strength of the electromagnet depends on the current and the number of turns on the coil.   [2]

....

....

....

2 Discuss whether your results are in agreement with:
   (a) Faraday's law   [1]

....

....

....

(b) Lenz's law [1]

....

....

....

Evaluation

How could the experiments be improved to give more reliable results? [2]

....

....

....

Extension

1 Sketch the magnetic field lines round a solenoid. [1]

2 A straight wire is held horizontally between a person's left and right hands. Use Fleming's right hand rule to determine which way current will flow in the wire when it is moved upwards through a magnetic field directed perpendicular to the wire and towards the person. [1]

....

4.6 Electric motor

Aim

To measure the efficiency of an electric motor.

Theory

- The efficiency of a device is defined by:

$$\text{efficiency} = \frac{\text{power output, } P_o}{\text{power input, } P_i} \times 100\%$$

where power, $P = \dfrac{\text{energy transfer or work done}}{\text{time taken}}$

- The rate at which electrical energy is transferred to a device, P_i, is given by:

$$P_i = IV$$

where I is the current through the device and V is the p.d. across it.
- The rate at which work is done by a motor in lifting a mass, m, through a height, h, in time, t, through a gravitational field of strength, g, is given by:

$$P_o = \frac{mgh}{t}$$

Apparatus

- ☐ 9 V battery
- ☐ ammeter (0–2 A)
- ☐ voltmeter (0–10 V)
- ☐ small electric motor
- ☐ string
- ☐ 100 g masses
- ☐ timer
- ☐ metre rule
- ☐ clamp
- ☐ wires and connectors

Procedure

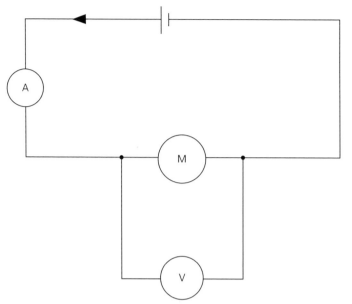

Figure 1

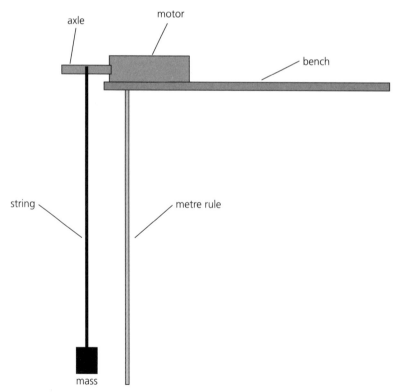

Figure 2

1   Connect the battery, ammeter and electric motor in series as shown in Figure 1.

2   Connect the voltmeter across the terminals of the electric motor.

3   Attach a 100g mass to the axle of the motor with a piece of string and allow the mass to hang freely over the edge of the bench (Figure 2). Clamp the motor to the bench.

4   Support the metre rule vertically behind the hanging mass.

5   Start the motor and record the time, t, it takes for the mass, m, to rise smoothly through a height, h, of 0.5m; record the ammeter and voltmeter readings while the mass is rising.

6   Increase the load by 100g and repeat step **5**.

7   Repeat step **6** two more times.

Method

Mention measurements and observations made, difficulties encountered and precautions taken to achieve good results.   [2]

....

....

....

....

....

....

....

....

....

....

Results and calculations

Complete Tables 1 and 2.

Table 1

I/A	V/V	IV/W	m/kg	h/m	mgh/J	t/s	mgh/t / W

[8]

Table 2

m/kg	Input power, P_i/W	Output power, P_o/W	Efficiency, $\dfrac{P_o}{P_i} \times 100\%$

[4]

Conclusions

Summarise and discuss your results for the efficiency of the electric motor. [2]

....

....

....

....

Is the efficiency of the motor affected by the size of the load?

....

Is the speed of the motor affected by the size of the load?

....

Where is energy lost?

....

....

....

....

Evaluation

Discuss how the experiment could be improved. [1]

....

....

....

Extension

1   A straight wire is held horizontally between a person's left and right hands; a current
flows in the wire from left to right and a magnetic field is directed perpendicular to
the wire and towards the person. Use Fleming's left hand rule to determine whether
the wire will move up or down. [1]

....

2   What factors influence the speed at which the coil rotates in an electric motor (in the
absence of a load)? [2]

....

....

....

....

....

....

5 Atomic physics

No practical experiments are provided for this chapter but see the Maltese cross experiment on page 137 for a demonstration of the effect of a magnetic field on a beam of elections. Investigations of the ionising effect and the relative penetrating power of alpha, beta and gamma radiation are described on pages 230–231 of *IGCSE Physics* (3rd edition, Duncan and Kennett). Discuss with your teacher the current developments and emerging research in this area.

More experiments

Ripple tank experiments

A ripple tank can be used to study the reflection, refraction and diffraction of water waves.

- It consists of a transparent tray, containing water to a depth of about 5 mm, with a light source above and a white screen below on which images of the waves are projected.
- The wave motion is studied more easily by using a stroboscope – a disc with a number of equally spaced slits in it. When the disc rotates at a speed such that each time a view of the screen is obtained the waves have advanced one wavelength, the waves appear to be 'frozen' or stationary.

 Warning!
People with epilepsy can be affected adversely by stroboscopic lighting. Before using a stroboscope, check that no one in the class is likely to be affected.

Ripples are produced by dipping into the water repeatedly.

- If a straight bar is attached to an electric motor, as shown in the diagram, continuous ripples are generated.
- Circular ripples are generated if the bar is replaced by a small ball.

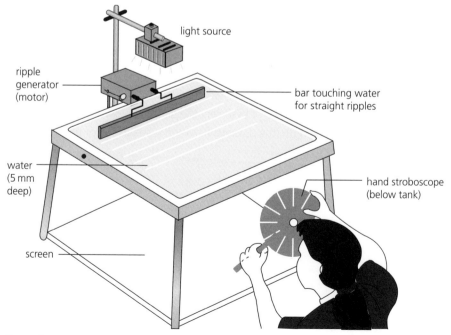

Figure 1

Reflection

1   Generate some continuous straight waves in the ripple tank. Place a straight metal strip in the tank at an angle of about 60° to the wave fronts and observe the reflection of the waves.

2   Make a sketch of the image obtained on the screen; the wave fronts are represented by the straight lines and can be regarded as the crests of waves.

3   Measure the angle of incidence, i, and the angle of reflection, r, of the wave fronts on the metal strip.
    •   Do the waves obey the law of reflection?

....

Refraction

1   Place a rectangular glass plate in the ripple tank; align it so that a straight edge is about 45° to the wave fronts. The plate should be of a thickness such that the depth of water above it is about 1 mm and about 5 mm elsewhere. Generate some continuous straight waves.

2   Make a sketch of the image obtained on the screen; the distance between the straight lines corresponds to the wavelength (the distance between wave crests) of the wave.

3   Measure the wavelength of the waves in the deep and shallow regions.

- Is the wavelength shorter or longer in the shallow region?

....

- In which region do the waves travel faster?

....

- What do you notice happens to the direction of travel of the waves as they enter the shallower water?

....

Diffraction

1 Place an obstacle with a gap in it of about the same wavelength as the water waves in the ripple tank as shown below.

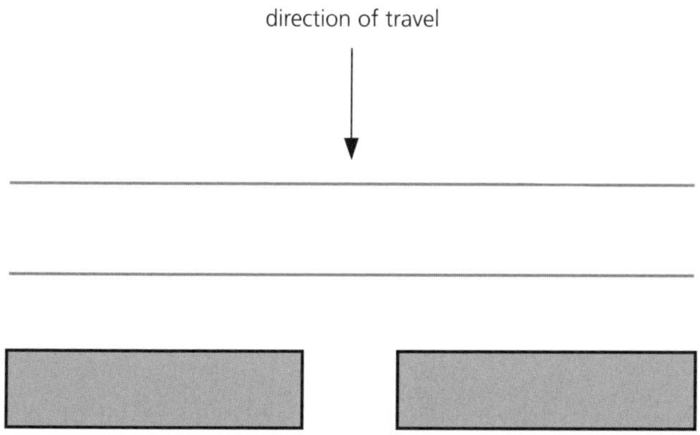

direction of travel

Figure 2

2 Make a sketch of the image obtained on the screen when continuous straight waves are incident on the gap.

- What happens to the waves when they pass through the gap?

....

3 Replace the obstacle with one having a much wider gap. Make a sketch of the image obtained on the screen when continuous straight waves are incident on the gap.

- What difference do you notice in the image from when a narrower gap was used?

....

Pressure due to the weight of a person

1 Stand on some bathroom scales and determine your mass: .... kg

2 Write down the force, *F*, you exert on the ground when standing:

.... N

3 Stand on a piece of graph paper and draw around the outline of one foot; count up the squares on the graph paper and estimate the contact area this foot has with the ground:

.... m^2

Total contact area of two feet on ground, *A* = ... m^2

4 Calculate the pressure, *p*, you exert on the ground from the formula:

$$p = \frac{F}{A}$$

$p =$ .... $\dfrac{\text{N}}{\text{m}^2}$

$=$ .... Pa

Thermal capacity

The **thermal capacity** of a body is the quantity of heat needed to raise the temperature of the whole body by 1 °C.

Solid cylinders made of different materials are required for this investigation; aluminium, copper, steel and brass are readily available.

1   Determine the specific heat capacity, c, for each cylinder by using the procedure given in Experiment 2.1 or use the values given in the table.

Table 1

Metal	Specific heat capacity / J/(kg °C)	Mass of metal/kg	Thermal capacity / J/°C
aluminium	910		
copper	385		
brass	380		
steel	450		

2   Complete the table by measuring the mass of each cylinder and calculating its thermal capacity from the formula:

   thermal capacity = mass of cylinder × specific heat capacity

Convection

- Convection currents in a liquid can be demonstrated by dropping a few crystals of potassium permanganate down a tube into a beaker of water. The tube is then removed and the water is heated gently from below the crystals with a Bunsen burner. Purple streamers rise, showing the path of convection currents.
- Convection currents in air can be made visible using the apparatus shown below.

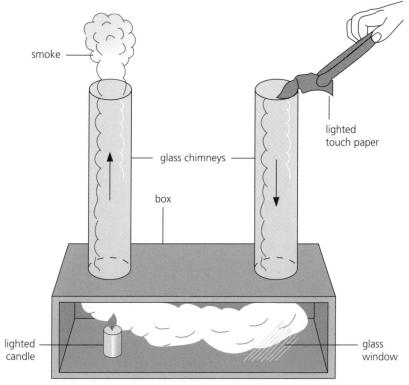

Figure 3

When the candle in the box is burning, convection currents are set up in the air, which are made visible by the smoke from the lighted touch paper.

Note: Ensure your lab has heat only fire alarms!

Rate of cooling

The rate of cooling of an object is proportional to the ratio of its surface area to its volume. This can be tested by pouring the same volume of hot water ($200\,cm^3$) into two beakers, one of which has a larger diameter than the other – a $250\,cm^3$ and a $500\,cm^3$ beaker are suitable. Record the temperature of the water in each beaker every 30 seconds to determine which cools fastest. A graph of temperature against time can be plotted for each.

Table 2

Time/s										
T_1/°C (small beaker)										
T_2/°C (large beaker)										

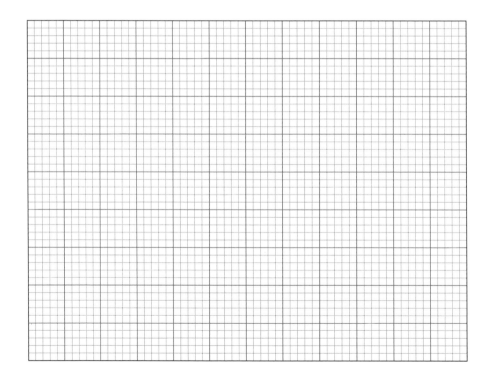

Gold-leaf electroscope

A gold-leaf electroscope can be used to detect charge and distinguish between good and bad conductors of electricity.

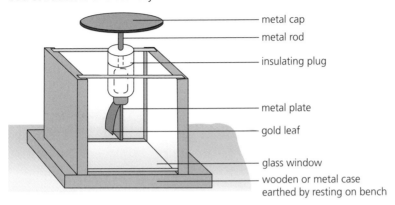

metal cap
metal rod
insulating plug
metal plate
gold leaf
glass window
wooden or metal case earthed by resting on bench

Figure 4

Charging and discharging a gold-leaf electroscope

1   Record below what happens to the gold leaf of the electroscope when:
    (a) a charged polythene rod is brought close to (but does not touch) the cap of an electroscope
    (b) the charged polythene rod is moved away from the electroscope
    (c) a charged acetate strip is brought close to the cap of the electroscope
    (d) the charged acetate strip is moved away from the electroscope
    (e) a charged polythene rod is drawn firmly across the edge of the cap of the electroscope.

2   Repeat step **1(e)** to charge the electroscope. Touch the cap of the charged electroscope with your finger.

3   Repeat step **1(e)** to charge the electroscope. Touch the cap of the charged electroscope with different materials such as plastic, metal and wood; if the gold leaf falls *quickly* the material is a good conductor.

4   Complete the following sentences, and the table.
    (a) When a charged polythene rod is brought near the electroscope cap the

      gold leaf ....
    (b) When the charged polythene rod is then moved away from the electroscope cap

      the gold leaf ....
    (c) When a charged cellulose acetate strip is brought near the electroscope cap the

      gold leaf ....

(d) When the charged acetate strip is then moved away from the electroscope cap the

gold leaf ....

(e) When a charged polythene rod is drawn across the edge of the electroscope cap

the gold leaf .... and the electroscope ....

(f) When you touch the charged electroscope cap with a finger, the gold leaf

.... and the electroscope ....

Table 3

Material	Gold leaf discharges quickly/slowly	Good/bad conductor

5 Explain how a gold-leaf electroscope can be used

(a) to detect charge

....

....

....

(b) to distinguish between conductors and insulators.

....

....

....

6 List the materials which you found to be good and bad conductors.

....

....

....

Maltese cross

The effect of a magnetic field on a beam of charged particles can be studied with a Maltese cross tube.

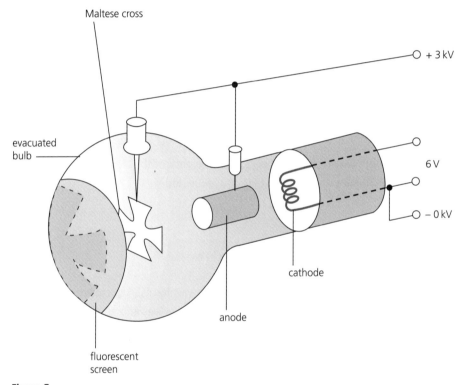

Figure 5

This is an evacuated glass tube with a fluorescent screen at one end and a 'Maltese cross' suspended in front of the screen. A cathode is heated and produces cathode rays that travel towards the anode; most pass through the hole in the anode and travel along the tube towards the cross. Those that do not strike the cross continue towards the screen and cause it to fluoresce with green or blue light; a shadow of the cross is cast on the screen.

1 Connect up the power supplies to the Maltese cross tube and adjust the settings to obtain a shadow of the cross on the fluorescent screen. It will help to see the shadow if the lights in the laboratory are dimmed.

• How do we know that the cathode rays travel in straight lines?

....

....

....

2 To observe the deflection of cathode rays in a magnetic field, bring the north pole of a bar magnet close to the neck of the tube so that the rays and the fluorescent shadow move upwards. (Note that the optical shadow of the cross, due to light emitted by the heated cathode, does not move and is unaffected by the magnetic field.)

• Use Fleming's left hand rule to determine the direction of the current in the tube and hence the charge on the cathode rays.

....

....

3 Now bring the south pole of the magnet close to the neck of the tube.

• In which direction are the cathode rays now deflected?

....

Cathode ray oscilloscope

A cathode ray oscilloscope (CRO) can be used to display waveforms. A microphone and tuning forks or a signal generator are used to convert sound waves into an electrical signal which is displayed on the CRO.

1 Switch on the CRO and adjust the focus and brightness of the trace to be sharp and of low intensity. Make sure the trig level setting is in the auto position.

2 Adjust the time base control so that a horizontal line is obtained on the screen of the CRO.

3 Adjust the Y-shift control so that the horizontal line is in the centre of the screen.

4 Attach a microphone to the Y-input and switch it on.

5 Sound a tuning fork close to the microphone and adjust the time base setting until two or three complete waves are seen on the screen; you may need to change the Y-amp gain so that both the peaks and troughs of the wave are displayed on the screen.

6 Sketch the appearance of the wave.

7 Repeat steps **5** to **6** using a tuning fork of different pitch. Do not alter the time base setting or the y-amp gain.

8 Sketch the appearance of the wave from the second tuning fork.

9 Investigate the effect of loudness on the amplitude of the waves. Instead of the tuning forks, a signal generator can be used to produce different sound frequencies.

Note: Instead of a CRO, a data-logger and computer with software which simulates the display on a CRO screen (by plotting the p.d. against time) can be used for this experiment.

First tuning fork

Sketch the waveform. [2]

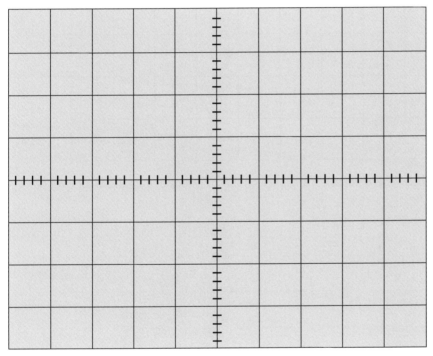

Second tuning fork

Sketch the waveform. [2]

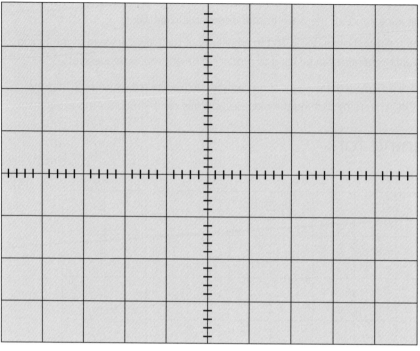

Summarise the effects of loudness and pitch on the amplitude and frequency of a sound.

....

....

....

....

....

....

1   In this experiment you will investigate the cooling of thermometer bulbs under different conditions.

Carry out the following instructions referring to Figures 1.1, 1.2 and 1.3.

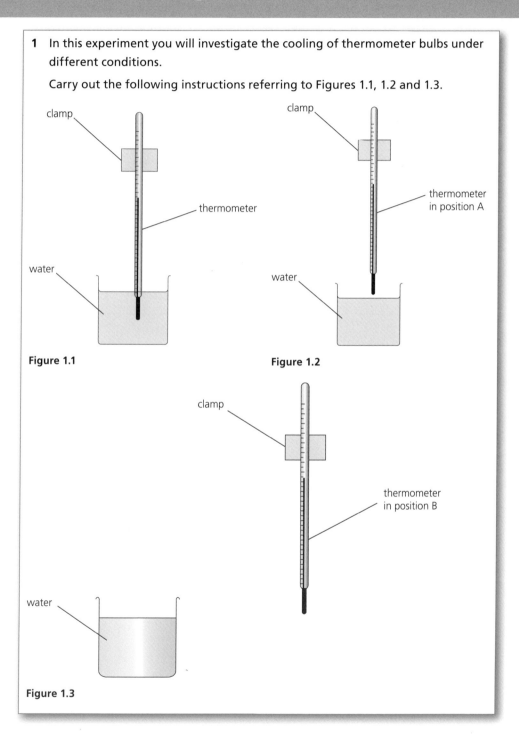

clamp

thermometer

water

Figure 1.1

clamp

thermometer in position A

water

Figure 1.2

clamp

thermometer in position B

water

Figure 1.3

(a) Place the thermometer in the beaker of hot water (see Figure 1.1).

    (i) Record the temperature θ_h of the hot water.

       θ_h = ...   [1]

    (ii) Move the thermometer until the thermometer bulb is just above the surface of the water (position **A**) as shown in Figure 1.2 and immediately start the stopclock.

    (iii) After 30 s measure the temperature θ shown on the thermometer. Record the time t (30 s) and the temperature reading in Table 1.1.

    (iv) Continue recording the time and temperature readings every 30 s until you have six sets of readings.

Table 1.1

t/	Position A, θ/	Position B, θ/

[5]

(b) Complete the column headings in the table.

(c) Replace the thermometer in the beaker of hot water and record its temperature.

    θ_h= ....   [1]

(d) Move the thermometer at least 10 cm away from the beaker to position **B** as shown in Figure 1.3 and immediately start the stopclock.

    (i) After 30 s measure the temperature θ shown on the thermometer. Record the temperature reading in Table 1.1.

    (ii) Continue recording the temperature every 30 s until you have six sets of readings.

(e) State in which position the thermometer bulb cooled more quickly. Justify your answer by reference to your readings.   [1]

    Statement ....

    Justification ....

    ....

(f) To make a fair comparison between the rates of cooling of the thermometer bulbs in the two positions it is important to control other experimental conditions. Suggest two conditions that should be controlled in this experiment. [2]

....

....

[Total: 10]

(Cambridge IGCSE Physics 0625, Paper 5 Q2, November 2009)

2 In this experiment you will determine the focal length of a converging lens by two different methods.

Method 1

Carry out the following instructions referring to Figure 2.1 and Figure 2.2.

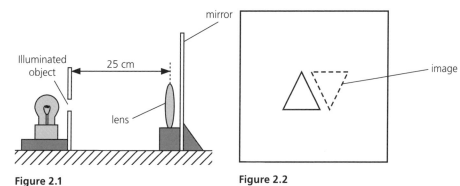

Figure 2.1   Figure 2.2

(a) Place the lens about 25 cm from the object screen and close to the mirror as shown in Figure 2.1.

(b) Move the lens and the mirror slowly towards the object screen until a sharply focused image is obtained on the object screen as shown in Figure 2.2.

(c) Measure the distance between the lens and the object screen. This distance is equal to the focal length *f* of the converging lens. Record *f* below.

f = ... [2]

Method 2

Carry out the following instructions referring to Figure 2.3.

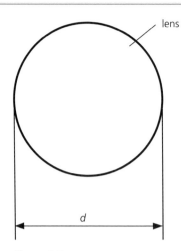

Figure 2.3

(d) Remove the lens from its holder. By placing the lens on the metre rule, determine an average value for the diameter *d* of the lens. Record your readings in the space below.

d = ... [3]

(e) Using the two blocks of wood and the metre rule determine the thickness *t* of the lens.

t = ... [1]

(f) Draw a diagram to show how you used the two blocks of wood and the metre rule with the lens. [2]

(g) (i) Theory shows that for a perfectly formed lens the focal length is given by the formula:

$$f = \frac{d^2}{kt}$$

where $k = 4.16$

Calculate the focal length f of the lens using this formula.

$f =$ .... [1]

(ii) Explain whether your results from Methods 1 and 2 support this theory. [1]

....

....

....

[Total: 10]

(Cambridge IGCSE Physics 0625, Paper 5 Q4, November 2009)

3 In this experiment, you are to determine the position of the centre of mass of an object using a balancing method.

Carry out the following instructions referring to Figure 3.1.

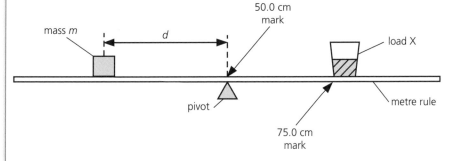

Figure 3.1

The load **X** has been taped to the metre rule so that one side of the base is exactly on the 75.0 cm mark. Do not move this load.

(a) Place a mass m of 30 g on the rule and adjust its position so that the rule is as near as possible to being balanced with the 50.0 cm mark exactly over the pivot as shown in Figure 3.1.

(i) Record in Table 3.1 the distance d from the centre of the 30 g mass to the 50.0 cm mark on the rule.

(ii) Repeat step (i) using masses of 40 g, 50 g, 60 g and 70 g to obtain a total of five sets of readings. Record the readings in the table.

(iii) For each value of d calculate $\frac{1}{d}$ and enter the values in the table.

Table 3.1

m/g	d/cm	$\frac{1}{d}$ / $\frac{1}{cm}$
30		
40		
50		
60		
70		

[2]

(b) Plot a graph of $\frac{m}{g}$ (y-axis) against $\frac{1}{d}$ / $\frac{1}{cm}$ (x-axis). [4]

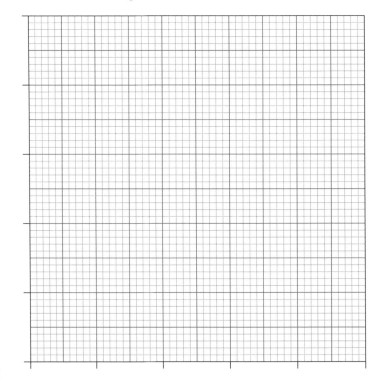

(c) Determine the gradient G of the graph. Show clearly on the graph how you obtained the necessary information.

$G =$ .... [2]

(d) Determine the horizontal distance z from the 75.0 cm mark on the rule to the centre of mass of the load **X** using the equation:

$$z = \frac{G - k}{x}$$

where $k = 1250$ g cm and $x = 50$ g

$z =$ .... [2]

[Total: 10]

(Cambridge IGCSE Physics 0625, Paper 51 Q1, November 2010)

4 In this experiment, you will investigate the current in resistors in a circuit.

Carry out the following instructions referring to Figure 4.1. The circuit is set up for you.

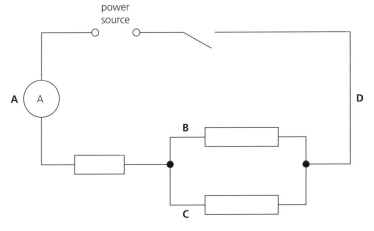

Figure 4.1

(a) (i) Switch on. Record the current I_A in the circuit.

I_A = ...

Switch off.

(ii) Change the position of the ammeter to the position marked **B** on Figure 4.1. Switch on. Record the current I_B in the circuit.

I_B = ...

Switch off.

(iii) Change the position of the ammeter to the position marked **C** on Figure 4.1. Switch on. Record the current I_C in the circuit.

I_C = ...

Switch off.

(iv) Change the position of the ammeter to the position marked **D** on Figure 4.1. Switch on. Record the current I_B in the circuit.

I_D = ...   [4]

Switch off.

(b) Theory suggests that $I_A = I_B + I_C$ and $I_D = I_B + I_C$.

   (i) Calculate $I_B + I_C$.

$I_B + I_C$ = ...

   (ii) State whether your experimental results support the theory and justify your statement by reference to your results.   [3]

statement ....

justification...

....

(c) (i) Connect the voltmeter so that it measures the potential difference *V* across the combination of the three resistors. Record the potential difference *V*.

V = ...

(ii) Calculate the resistance *R* of the combination of the three resistors using the equation $R = \dfrac{V}{I}$.

R = ...   [2]

(d) On Figure 4.1, draw in the voltmeter connected as described in **(c)(i)** using the standard symbol for a voltmeter.   [1]

[Total: 10]

(Cambridge IGCSE Physics 0625, Paper 51 Q3, November 2011)

1 The IGCSE class is investigating the stretching of springs.

Each student is able to use a selection of different springs, a set of slotted masses to hang on the end of a spring, a metre rule, and any other common laboratory apparatus that may be useful.

A student decides to investigate the effect of the type of metal from which the spring is made on the extension produced by loading the spring.

(a) Suggest three possible variables that should be kept constant in this investigation. (Do not include variables that are likely to have very little effect on the length of a spring in this context.) [3]

1 ....

2 ....

3 ....

(b) In the investigation, the original length l_0 of a spring is measured and then the new length l when a load is attached. Figure 1.1 shows an unloaded spring and the same spring with a load attached. On Figure 1.1, show clearly the original length l_0 and the new length l. [1]

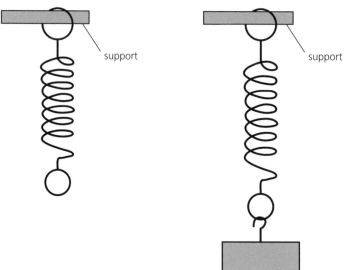

support

support

Figure 1.1

(c) It is not possible to position a metre rule immediately next to the spring. Describe briefly how you would overcome this problem when measuring the length *l*. You may draw a diagram. [1]

....

....

[Total: 5]

(Cambridge IGCSE Physics 0625, Paper 63 Q5, November 2010)

2 The IGCSE class is studying the acceleration of a toy car that is pulled along a track by a force *F*.

The arrangement is shown in Figure 2.1.

Figure 2.1

A student uses a force *F* of 0.5 N to pull a toy car along a track and electronically measures the acceleration *a*. He records the result in a table. He repeats the procedure using a range of different forces up to 2.5 N. The readings are shown in Table 2.1.

Table 2.1

$\dfrac{F}{N}$	$\dfrac{a}{m/s^2}$
0.5	0.35
1.0	0.72
1.5	1.02
2.0	1.44
2.5	1.74

(a) Plot a graph of $\dfrac{F}{N}$ (*y*-axis) against $\dfrac{a}{\text{m/s}^2}$ (*x*-axis).   [5]

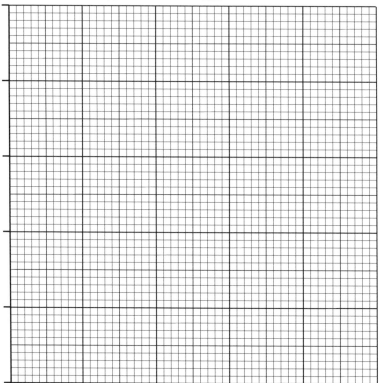

(b) Theory suggests that the acceleration is directly proportional to the force applied to the toy car. State whether the results support this suggestion and justify your statement by reference to the graph.   [2]

Statement ....

Justification ....

....

(c) The gradient of the graph is equal to the mass of the toy car. From the graph, determine the mass *m* of the toy car. Show clearly how you obtained the necessary information.

m = ...   [3]

[Total: 10]

(Cambridge IGCSE Physics 0625, Paper 63 Q1, November 2010)

3 An IGCSE student is investigating the passage of light through a transparent block using optics pins.

The student's ray trace sheet is shown in Figure 3.1.

The student places two pins P_1 and P_2 to mark the incident ray. He looks through the block and places two pins P_3 and P_4 to mark the emergent ray so that P_3, P_4 and the images of P_1 and P_2 appear to be exactly one behind the other. He draws the outline of the block. He removes the block and pins and draws in the incident ray and the emergent ray.

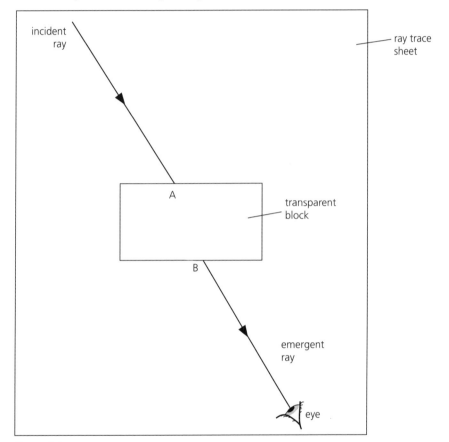

Figure 3.1

(a) (i) On Figure 3.1, mark suitable positions for the four pins. Label the pins P_1, P_2, P_3 and P_4.

(ii) Draw the normal at point **A**. [2]

(b) (i) Draw in the line **AB**. Measure and record the angle of refraction r between the line **AB** and the normal.

$r =$ ....

(ii) Measure and record the angle of incidence i between the incident ray and the normal.

$i =$ ....   [2]

(c) The student does not have a set square or any other means to check that the pins are vertical. Suggest how he can ensure that his P_3 and P_4 positions are as accurate as possible.   [1]

....

....

[Total: 5]

(Cambridge IGCSE Physics 0625, Paper 63 Q1, November 2011)

4 The IGCSE class is investigating the resistance of a wire.

The circuit is shown in Figure 4.1.

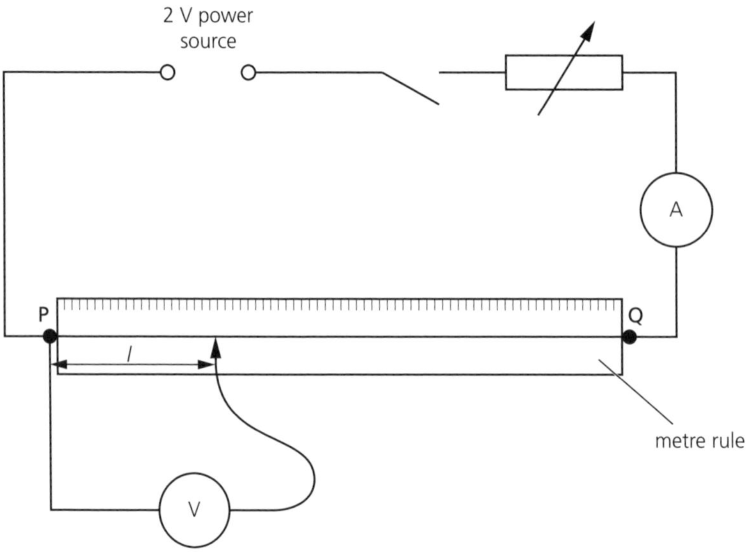

Figure 4.1

(a) A student measures and records in Table 4.1 the current *I* in the circuit and the potential difference *V* across a length *l* = 0.250 m of wire **PQ**.

She repeats the procedure using *l* values of 0.500 m and 0.750 m.

 (i) Complete the heading for each column of the table.

 (ii) Calculate the resistance *R* of each length *l* of the wire using the equation $R = \dfrac{V}{I}$. Record the value of *R* in the table.

Table 4.1

I/	V/	I/	R/
0.250	0.54	0.32	
0.500	1.10	0.32	
0.750	1.61	0.32	

[4]

(b) Use numbers from the table to suggest and justify a relationship between the length *l* of the wire and its resistance *R*. Show your working.

 relationship

 ....

 justification [3]

 ....

 ....

(c) Use the results to predict the resistance of a 1.50 m length of the same wire. Show your working.

 prediction .... [2]

(d) Another student proposes that the accuracy of the experiment would be improved by using a 12 V power source.

Suggest two effects that this might have on the experiment. [2]

1.

....

2.

....

[Total: 11]

(Cambridge IGCSE Physics 0625, Paper 63 Q3, November 2011)